Breakthrough

How to Build a Million Dollar Business by Helping Others Succeed

By:

King Pinyin

This book is designed to provide information that the author believes to be accurate on the subject matter it covers, but it is sold with the understanding that neither the author nor the publisher is offering individualized advice tailored to any specific business or to any individual's particular needs, or rendering advice or other professional services. A competent professional's services should be sought if one needs expert assistance.

Every effort has been made to make all publications and products sold through this site or through phone and mail as complete and accurate as possible. However, there may be mistakes both typographical and in content. Therefore, this text should be used only as a general guide and not as the ultimate reference source.

This publication references data and experiences collected over many time periods. Past results do not guarantee future performance. This book solely provides historical data to discuss and illustrate the underlying principles. Additionally, this book is not intended to serve as the basis for any financial decision.

No warranty is made with respect to the accuracy or completeness of the information contained herein, and both the author and the publisher specifically disclaim any responsibility for any liability, loss, or risk, personal or otherwise, which is incurred as a consequence, directly or indirectly, of the use and application of any of the contents of this book.

Praise for King Pinyin

"All successful network marketers share a common trait; that is an overwhelming desire and commitment to succeed. The road up to the highest levels in the network marketing industry is covered with unexpected roadblocks, uphill climbs and detours. It is not a business for the faint-of-heart or for people who are looking for an easy path to wealth. I have witnessed one of our most successful leaders, King Pinyin, overcome seemingly insurmountable obstacles in her climb to the top of our company. From the very first day I met King at a meeting in Birmingham, Alabama, I knew she had the drive and passion necessary to be a superstar in our organization. With no prior experience, she built a multinational team that continues to be a force in our company. As a natural outgrowth, she has become a powerful motivational speaker and success coach who is impacting lives around the world."

Craig Jerabeck
President & CEO
5LINX Enterprises, Inc.

"I'm always thrilled by King's drive, passion, enthusiasm and commitment to excellence in everything she does. They are so strong you can literally feel and touch them. This book will ignite the breakthrough habits of success into the hearts and minds of the readers."

Valentine Ozigbo
Managing Director/Chief Executive Officer
Transcorp Hotels Plc.

"King has helped thousands of professionals in their direct selling business. Her expertise and results are a perfect reflection of her relentless spirit to maximize her potential and make a difference in the world. Her words will not only educate and equip you, but will also ignite your greater passion and purpose in life and business!"

Melissa West
International Success Coach, Trainer, Speaker
Author, Your Daily W.O.W.

"King was first a student with a relentless passion to learn how to be the best in the business. Once she succeeded at the highest level, she has been inspired to share her drive for success with others and showing the power of possibilities."

Jason Guck
Executive Vice President Sales
5LINX Enterprises Inc

"What I admire most about King is her ability to courageously transform her life to limitless heights, and then most importantly sharing those lessons from her experience with the world!"

Elizabeth Muna
Independent Senior National Sales Director (NSD)
Mary Kay Cosmetics
1st African born NSD in 50yrs of Mary Kay USA history!

"For nine years, I have watched King Pinyin's growth as a leader in this industry. I must say it is impressive. From her early days, when she would travel for hours to learn from a documented leader, she has been an aggressive student of success, and has shown true tenacity and perseverance. She has been mentored by some of the best leaders in the world, and now has chosen to share what she has learned. I believe that anyone can utilize this as a guidebook to reach the highest levels of direct marketing."

William Faucette, Jr.
Vice-President, North American Sales
5LINX Enterprises, Inc.

"King Pinyin is an engaging, action-oriented speaker with a powerful message for entrepreneurs. King knows what it takes to build and run a multi-million dollar business and she openly shares personal business successes and challenges to help you to be successful. This is more than a motivational book, but a realistic and life changing transcript to your Breakthrough."

Barry L Donalson, CDSP
Entrepreneur, Author, Business Coach
Million Dollar Earner

"I am honored to have known King over the last few years and been a part of her success journey. King's commitment to personal growth and sharing her knowledge with others is exceptional. King has an in your face, hold you accountable approach with the perfect amount of Christian love and support. She is an incredible mentor to many and an anointed woman of God. Here's to the Breakthrough!"

Lisa Nicole Cloud-Naugles
Entrepreneur, Success Coach, Philanthropist
Million Dollar Earner

"A very inspiring book with relevant success strategies about how to turn dreams into a reality. I am confident that the information in this book will empower you in the pursuit of your deepest purpose."

Nganje Kinge Monono
Finance Counselor
Cameroon Permanent Mission to the United Nations, NY

"I feel that King Pinyin is one of the most determined women I've ever met. Once she sets her mind on something it will most surely happen. Her loving spirit and giving heart is one characteristic that sets her apart and makes her one of the phenomenal women I know."

Rosa Battle
Entrepreneur, Speaker, Success Coach
Author, Walking in Your Success

"I love studying books by authors who have practiced the principles they teach. This is definitely a book to study."

Nnamdi Jarrod Wilkins-Agomo
Entrepreneur, Transformational Teacher
Organo Gold Diamond

"It's rare that you meet someone who can put a thought in their head and bring it to life. I have had the pleasure of watching King's relentless spirit and how she brings life into any room she steps into. Her faith and ambition alone is a good reason to learn from a woman of her stature and caliber."

Tishina Anderson
Trainer, Mentor, Success Coach
Million Dollar Earner

Who Are Your Mentors... Proximity Is POWER!

I am a woman in process. I'm just trying like everybody else. I try to take every conflict, every experience, and learn from it. Life is never dull.

— *Oprah Winfrey*

The greatest discovery of all time is that a person can change his future by merely changing his attitude. — *Oprah Winfrey*

"I've come to believe that all my past failure and frustration were actually laying the foundation for the understandings that have created the new level of living I now enjoy."

— *Anthony Robbins*

"In essence, if we want to direct our lives, we must take control of our consistent actions. It's not what we do once in a while that shapes our lives, but what we do consistently." — *Anthony Robbins*

"Leadership is not about titles, positions or flowcharts. It is about one life influencing another." — *John C. Maxwell*

"A man must be big enough to admit his mistakes, smart enough to profit from them, and strong enough to correct them." — *John C. Maxwell*

"The greatest day in your life and mine is when we take total responsibility for our attitudes. That's the day we truly grow up." — *John C. Maxwell*

"Doubt and fear steal more dreams than failure does."

—*Darren Hardy*

"The difficulties of life are intended to make us better, not bitter."

—*Darren Hardy*

"Champions have the courage to keep turning the pages because they know a better chapter lies ahead."

— *Pastor Paula White*

"You have to love what you do. The difference between failure and success is 1%". — *Jeb Tyler*

"No one can keep you down unless you allow it. Make a decision, then burn the boats. Make your dream happen!"

— *Craig Jerabeck*

"Based on the struggles that I've been through, when we say representatives come first you can count on it!" — *Craig Jerabeck*

"You will only be remembered for two things: the problems you solve or the ones you create"

— *Dr. Mike Murdock*

"There is nothing in your destiny, nothing in your future that you cannot accomplish."

— *Larry King*

"I didn't learn anything while I was talking."

— *Larry King*

"Everything that happens to you is a reflection of what you believe about yourself. We cannot outperform our level of self-esteem. We cannot draw to ourselves more than we think we are worth." — *Iyanla Vanzant*

"Your willingness to look at your darkness is what empowers you to change."

—*Iyanla Vanzant*

"It's not what you say out of your mouth that determines your life, it's what you whisper to yourself that has the most power!"

— *Robert T. Kiyosaki*

"Winners are not afraid of losing. But losers are. Failure is part of the process of success. People who avoid failure also avoid success."

— *Robert T. Kiyosaki*

Dedication

To all those who believe in free enterprise but are struggling to find balance between career, family, relationships, personal time and building a dynamic million dollar business. You can do it!

And to Melai, Denzel, Precious, Makayla, Ulric, Yva, Jayden, Isidore & Illia. You guys are my favorite people in the whole wide world! I love you.

Table of Contents

FOREWORD BY JEB TYLER EXECUTIVE VICE PRESIDENT, MARKETING 5LINX ENTERPRISES INC. 16

INTRODUCTION   18

PART I: NETWORK MARKETING AND THE AMERICAN DREAM 24

CHAPTER 1: GETTING STARTED 26

CHAPTER 2: WHY THE BUZZ?   34

CHAPTER 3: CHOOSING THE RIGHT COMPANY   44

CHAPTER 4: UNDERSTANDING THE IMPORTANCE OF USING SYSTEMS IN DIRECT SALES   50

PART II: BUSINESS BUILDING ACTIVITIES   55

CHAPTER 5: THE RECRUITING PROCESS   57

CHAPTER 6: HOW TO BECOME A MASTER PRESENTER   69

CHAPTER 7: CUSTOMER ACQUISITION AND RETENTION   85

CHAPTER 8: GROWING YOUR BUSINESS THROUGH EVENTS   92

CHAPTER 9: UNDERSTANDING THE TEAM BUILDING GAME   107

PART III: PERSONAL GROWTH AND DEVELOPMENT   116

CHAPTER 10: SEVEN FIGURE INCOME EARNER MINDSET   118

CHAPTER 11: IT'S ALL ABOUT TAKING OWNERSHIP OF YOUR BUSINESS   132

CHAPTER 12: EFFECTIVE LEADERSHIP STRATEGIES   145

PIECING IT ALL TOGETHER   151

ACKNOWLEDGMENTS   159

ABOUT THE AUTHOR   158

ADDITIONAL RESOURCES   161

RECOMMENDED READING: 164

When you put your whole heart into it the dream will take you places you've never been before.

www.kingpinyin.com

Foreword

I have had the utmost pleasure of working very closely with King Pinyin for many years. She has been very instrumental in the growth of our company both in the U.S and internationally. The story of King's rise to success in the direct sales, motivational speaking and coaching industries is one of hard work, dedication and commitment to personal and professional growth at the highest level. When I first met King back in 2005, her story was the story of most Americans today. She was still working in corporate America as a database administrator and building her business alongside her job on a part-time basis. She had never owned a business before and she had no clue how far her new venture would take her. But one thing that stood out about King was her passion and enthusiasm to change her life using 5LINX as a vehicle. She knew for a fact that she was not going to live the life she wanted if she stayed on that career path.

What has impressed me the most about King is the tremendous amount of personal growth she has experienced since we first met back in 2005. King recognized right away that to be successful you need to mentor under successful people in your field of interest. She was relentless in her thirst for knowledge about the direct sales industry and about the company she had just joined. If you ever get a chance to work directly with King you'll come to understand that she does not accept no or failure as an option in life and business. If you looked up the word 'persistence' in the dictionary, you'll see King Pinyin staring back at you! That's my running joke with King because there's no turning back once she puts her mind into doing something. And she does it with so much heart and attention to details so much so that I have come to trust, respect and depend upon King's opinion on many things.

Like so many people who have experienced success, King went through a lot of setbacks before achieving her goals and dreams. I've watched King and her husband Sunny rebuild their sales organization with our company at least twice in the last 9years where many other leaders would have simply given up. And what's remarkable about both setbacks is King's ability to withdraw into herself in order to key into the reason for the setback. That's a classic mark of a true leader. Because King walks her talk, now she is a mentor to thousands all over the world and is a legend in her industry.

This book will give you a thorough insight into the direct sales industry and how you can start and grow your own business with a very low investment that can potentially produce huge returns. If you have a strong desire to make a change in your life and in your business, follow the path of success that King Pinyin has laid out for you in this book. She has helped thousands of people start their own business and she can help you as well.

Jeb Tyler
Executive Vice President, Marketing
5LINX Enterprises Inc.

Introduction

"We'll see you on Sunday at 7:00 p.m." With these few words, my husband, Sunny, committed us to attending a private business presentation in 2005. As a typical wife, my initial reaction was to let him know how inconsiderate he was for not checking with me first before accepting the invitation. I already had plans for Sunday night; and that did not include going anywhere for a business presentation. All I wanted to do was tuck my 2-year-old son, Denzel, into bed by 9:00 p.m. and then get myself ready for a very long and stressful week at work as a database administrator. But something very strange happened, just before I could say no to going anywhere with Sunny on that night. In one split second, I became overwhelmingly aware of the lack that was predominant in every area of our lives, and a deep yearning for something more completely engulfed me. In that moment of clarity it dawned on me that we would have to do something radically different from what we had been doing in order to experience life in a whole new way.

Our life back then was no different from most Americans. We were in a terrible place! We had 4 jobs between us, and still could not make ends meets. Money was incredibly tight, and our extended families depended on the little we had; the bills were always late and our self-esteem was at an all-time low. To crown it all, we had a 2-year-old son to take care of! Anyone who has had any experience with a 2-year-old child knows exactly what I'm talking about. You soon come to understand why they call that age the "terrible twos."

Needless to say, we argued a lot and our relationship began to fall apart. Living the American Dream for us had slowly become a nightmare. Like you, we both had big dreams about living happily-ever-after when we left college with those degrees! After all, like your parents, our parents insisted for years that getting a good education equaled getting a good job — which translated into a good life! Yea right! That is very true if you're just looking to get by in life.

However, I've found out over the last couple of years that if you desire to live like those people whom you admire (or secretly despise because they seem to have it all), you'll need a whole lot more than just a college education and a few degrees in your pocket. You'll need a strong desire to be more and have more than the hand that life has dealt you at the current moment. You must make a decision to go boldly in the direction of your big dreams regardless of the obstacles in your path. And boy there will be plenty!

You must also make a personal commitment to never stop trying until life bends in your favor, by cultivating a mind that's open to all the possibilities that exist in the universe. Additionally, you must have faith that your life has purpose and meaning. I'll talk more about how to achieve these states of mind in part 3 of this book.

And so it was that on the night of Sunday August 28th, 2005, we set off for the private business reception that will forever change our lives in Clarksville, Maryland. To be honest with you, the thought of going to a business presentation that late at night did not seem like such a terrible idea all of a sudden. Clarksville is a beautiful neighborhood with exquisite million dollar homes! I was looking forward to driving past those gorgeous mansions with perfectly manicured lawns, water fountains, and long driveways.

I don't know about you, but I love the finer things in life, and I often drove by and wondered what the folks who lived in those mansions did for a living! Then we pulled up into one of those long driveways and I suddenly had second thoughts. I knew that we had no business doing business with the type of people who lived in these homes.

My mind started playing a very old and familiar trick on me. It told me that the people living in that house were way beyond our league, and that I was a fool for believing that we could go into any kind of a business venture with them. Fear wanted me to back out from hearing the presentation, just like it had gripped and taken me over several times in the past. Besides, at 4:00 a.m. that morning I had to wake up to my alarm clock and get my 2-year-old ready for daycare and myself ready for work. As I wrestled with my thoughts, Sunny was already out of the car before I could express them. I guess he had sensed my hesitation and did not want to deal with any of my fears and doubts! I thank God every day for his decision. Reluctantly, I walked in with him. However, I made him promise to leave the house by 9:30 p.m. — even if the presentation was still going on. After all, I had to be at work early. Little did we know that our lives were about to be changed forever by that one phone call two days earlier, and Sunny's decision to say 'yes' to considering a business opportunity without checking with me!

I had never heard the term 'pyramid scheme', MLM, direct sales or network marketing before that day, and that turned out to be our saving grace! I had absolutely no clue that I could start and own a home-based business for less than a few hundred dollars! I had always assumed that starting a business was for the rich and famous who were lucky to have tens of thousands of dollars to invest. In my ignorance, I had counted ordinary people like myself out of the entrepreneurial game and doomed to working for the rest of them! But all of my preconceived notions were about to be changed that night.

We made the decision to move forward with the company based on the business concept that was explained to us in less than ninety minutes. The product portfolio was very diversified, and the compensation plan sounded very lucrative to us. We also inquired about the integrity and vision of the company founders and the type of support we could expect from our line of sponsorship and from the company leadership as a whole. Unfortunately, so many people have passed up on, or have been talked out of, a potentially good business opportunity just because some well-meaning (but poorly informed) family member or friend labeled it something else like "pyramid scheme," network marketing, or MLM.

Before we dive deeper into how to start and grow your own home-based business, I want to take a moment to encourage you to always trust your gut feelings. That's how God or the universe communicates with us. My own family would have stolen my dream of becoming a top earner in our industry had I not been aware of the importance of listening to the still small voice within me. That same voice is within you and waiting for you to shut off the third voices so that it can guide, guard and direct you toward your purpose.

We left the business reception that night at about 11:00 p.m. as brand new home-based business owners with big dreams and a strong desire to make them come true. We were, what I call today, "ignorance on fire" and we were on our way to the top of the compensation plan!

I could hardly wait for daybreak to share my new discovery with everyone I knew. I felt like I had stumbled on the best kept secret in America – the fact that anyone could start and grow a decent business from the luxury and comfort of their homes with very little money. Glory Halleluiah! The thought of having extra money in my bank account after all the bills and credit cards were paid every month was exhilarating!

I don't know if you can relate, but we had a broke date in my house. It was the 21st of the month! There was never any money left in either one of our bank accounts past that date! As a matter of fact, my card was declined that night for the initial investment of $499 and we had to borrow the startup fee from our friend!

As we went about sharing the business opportunity with friends and family, the business started growing, and so did the challenges too. A lot more people said no to us than they said yes, but that did not stop us from believing in what we had heard and knew about the possibilities in direct sales.

Beyond our wildest dream, the business income soon matched my full-time database administrator income in just ninety days, and then significantly surpassed it by our fourth month. I decided to quit my job and go full-time so that I could completely immerse myself into learning the business. We had our first 5-figure week shortly thereafter, and after seven months of learning, earning and growing with the business, Sunny decided to retire from his job. We were beside ourselves with happiness!

Our American Dream was finally becoming a reality! Nothing in the world felt better than not having to wake up to that alarm clock, and to letting my little boy wake up when he was fully rested. In nine months and with no prior experience, we reached the top position in the company.

In those early days of our career, all we had was a burning desire to succeed and a willingness to learn. I know that if you give your business all you've got, you can begin with the transformation process in your life too. I'm not just talking about financial transformation; the network marketing industry is (in my opinion) a personal development journey with a compensation plan. We have experienced growth in every area of our lives and have made many new friends, some of whom are our extended families now. We have been mentored by some of the best mentors and coaches, and have travelled the world. We have been able to give back to our family and causes that we believe in, all because we stepped out in faith on that August night in 2005.

After all these years in the direct sales industry and having earned a few million dollars, I have found out that success does not come to you, you go to it. If you are still reading this book, it means that you are someone who wants and deserves more from life. I commend you for that! Why? I believe that it is time for all of us to rise up to the challenges in our lives and take that bull called life by the horns and dance with it to the beat of our own drum!

The rules for success are the same across the board. In the chapters of this book, I will share all that I have learned over the years with you, so that you, too, can tell your story in the near future. If you are ever in doubt about yourself or your ability to rise to the top in any company of your choice, I want you to remember that many of us have done it with no experience at all, and so can you. I encourage you to get out of your own way, commit to being a student of your business and let me show you how to become a direct sales millionaire by helping others to succeed.

This book will go into detail about the direct sales industry, how to create a winning mindset, the goal-setting process, handling rejection, business building activities (including the recruiting process), developing effective presentation skills, the importance of a system, using events and social media to grow your business, team-building activities, what to do when your business hits a plateau, developing yourself as a leader and so much more.

In the end and as a result of reading this book, I hope that you feel equipped, encouraged and empowered to go boldly in the direction of your dreams. I'd like to be your friend, mentor and coach as you embark upon this new phase of your life.

It does not matter if this is your first home-based business or the tenth one, together we can start from today and create a new ending — an ending that will lead you to a place of financial, emotional, spiritual, mental, and physical abundance in your life and in your relationships. Let's stay connected through my website www.kingpinyin.com where you can have access to my blog, podcast, talk show interviews, videos and additional resources to help you grow from the inside out. I'm also very active on social media. I use Facebook daily to mentor and coach entrepreneurs. Feel free to connect with me via that means on facebook.com/emeldine. Text king pinyin to 55469 to be added to my free coaching program.

It's time to Illuminate and Shine!

Blessings,

King Pinyin

Part I

Network Marketing and
The American Dream

Stop waiting for the perfect moment to begin living the life you desire. That time may never come. Live in the eternal now.

www.kingpinyin.com

"In America, if you work hard and play by the rules, if you take responsibility for yourself and your family, you should have all the opportunity that you need for a better future. That's America's basic bargain and it's what the work of direct selling helps to promote each and every day. You strengthen our country and our economy, not just by striving for your own success, but by offering opportunity to others."

- President Bill Clinton (D)

Chapter 1

Getting Started

If you won the lottery today and wanted to build your dream house, what action steps would you take in order to make that dream a reality? If your response is to do your due diligence about the state, city, neighborhood and actual costs involved in building the house, then you have a 95% chance of not only building your dream house, but also enjoying the entire process before you call it a home. .

When my husband and I first started in the industry in the fall of 2005, we wanted to know everything about it. Everyone who knows me will tell you that when I commit myself to any endeavor, I do it wholeheartedly and with passion. Very rarely do I invest my time, money and energy in anything that I do not believe in wholeheartedly. I have found this to be true for a vast majority of successful people.

The number one cause of failure in the industry is, in my opinion, not a weak "why" like most people think. The number one cause of failure for the majority of people who get into the network marketing industry is a lack of knowledge about what direct selling is all about. If you think about it, most people hear about the industry from their friends and family members who heard about it from their friends and family members who, for the most part, just joined the business.

My husband, Sunny, and I received our introduction to the company by a very close friend who had been in the business for just a week. His uncle, who had also been in the business for only a week, introduced him to the business! Thank God we were fortunate enough to have had someone in our immediate line of sponsorship living in our city that had been with the company for a couple of months and had the drive of an entrepreneur. Many people who join network-marketing companies are not always lucky enough to have a leader nearby to lay the proper foundation. So, before we begin to talk about business-building activities, let's build a solid foundation first.

Direct Sales Industry

Direct selling encompasses a variety of distribution methods; **multilevel marketing (MLM)** or **network marketing** is one type of distribution and compensation method. In a multilevel distribution model, products and services are distributed from one level of distributorship to another and the compensation is based not only on your own product sales, but also on the product sales of the distributors in your business organization — also called your *downline*.

It is very important to note that direct sellers earn nothing for the mere recruitment others into the business. Individuals participate in direct selling in numerous ways, including purchasing products and services for personal use, referring customers to the company and/or retailing the products and services themselves or through their sales organizations.

Direct salespeople can be called *distributors, representatives, consultants, agents* or various other titles. An estimated **15.9 million people** are involved in direct selling in America and more than **90 million people** worldwide.

Number of People Involved in Direct Selling in the U.S.

The number of people involved in direct selling in the United States increased 1.9% to 15.9 million in 2012 from 15.6 million in 2011.

The industry experienced a surge of new direct selling independent representatives at the height of the recession. Due to normal attrition and the fact that some people join the industry for the short term, the slight reduction in force was expected in 2010 and 2011. The size of the industry's sales force is once again on the rise.

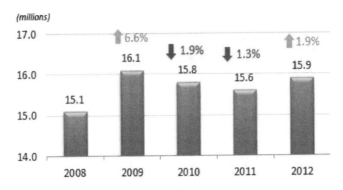

Note: These are estimated data based on survey data and extrapolated data from secondary sources.

Source: http://www.dsa.org/research/2012-industry-statistics

About 80 percent of U.S. direct sellers are women. This ought to make many women happy! The vast majority of them are independent business owners whose purpose is to sell the product and/or services of the company they voluntarily choose to represent. One thing that got me very excited about this industry is the fact that distributors do not work *for* the company but *with* the company. It's a very subtle difference, but it makes all the difference in the world.

Approximately 90 percent of all direct sellers operate their businesses from home, on a part-time basis. Even though it may not seem like a lucrative business model for those who are not involved, direct selling is a robust industry. U.S. sales totaled about **$31.6 billion in 2012**, with more than 74 percent of the American public having purchased goods or services through direct selling. How will your life change if you were positioned to earn just a tiny fraction of that amount in 2012? Worldwide sales are also strong with more than **$154 billion** in sales. (Source: Direct Selling Association)

2012 Estimated Direct Retail Sales* - (in Billions USD)

The 2012 estimated retail sales of USD 31.63 billion for the direct selling channel were up 5.9% in the United States, from USD 29.87 billion in 2011.

The U.S. market increase of 5.9% in 2012 accelerated an upward trend after bottoming out in 2009. Direct sales grew 0.8% in 2010 and 4.6% in 2011.

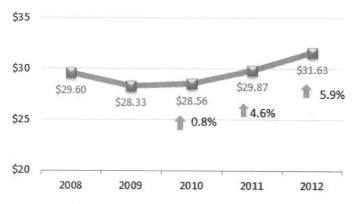

*Direct retail sales are defined as the dollar amount paid by the ultimate consumers of the products or services. These are estimated direct retail sales based on survey data and extrapolated data from secondary sources.

Source: http://www.dsa.org/research/2012-industry-statistics

Direct Selling Association

Every profession has a governing body. I was elated to find that network-marketing companies are no exception. The Direct Selling Association (DSA), headquartered in Washington, D.C., is the national trade association of the leading firms that manufacture and distribute goods and services sold directly to consumers by its distributors.

Approximately 200 companies are members of the association, including many well-known brand names. The Association's mission is *"To protect, serve and promote the effectiveness of member companies and the*

29

independent business people they represent. To ensure that the marketing by member companies of products and/or the direct sales opportunity is conducted with the highest level of business ethics and service to consumers." You may be surprised to know that many distributors living in and around the Washington, D.C. metro area are not even aware of the fact that the DSA is right in their backyard. In the beginning of our journey, we were able to weather the storms regarding the credibility of network marketing because we drove out to the DSA office in D.C., which also serves as the headquarters for the world federation of direct selling associations. They provided us with invaluable support and information. Find out more from www.dsa.org.

World Federation of Direct Selling Association

Not too many people are aware of the fact that network marketing is a worldwide business venture. The idea of starting a business from the luxury of your home and growing it into a worldwide business makes MLM very attractive for those involved in it.

If you are someone who loves to travel the world, then you may want to look into the direct sales industry. We have travelled the world and met so many people because of our network marketing business. Because of the global nature of the business model, the *World Federation of Direct Selling Associations (WFDSA)* was founded in 1979.

The WFDSA is a non-governmental, voluntary organization globally representing the direct selling industry as a federation of national Direct Selling Associations. Its membership consists of more than 60 national direct selling associations and one regional federation — the Federation of European Direct Selling Associations (Seldia). One delegate from each association, as well as a number of regional and global officers, serves as the Board of Directors. The headquarters for the WFDSA is the United States Direct Selling Association in Washington, D.C. I strongly encourage you to visit the office on K Street anytime you are in or around Washington, D.C. or visit the websites listed below for more information:

www.wfdsa.org

www.seldia.eu

www.directsellingfacts.com

www.directselling411.com

Benefits of Direct Selling

I could go on and on about why network marketing makes so much sense. Some of the most popular reasons why people choose direct selling include the following:

- **It is a good way to meet and socialize with people.** I have met some of the best people in the world through my business. Not surprisingly, many couples have met through building their businesses. So, if you're looking for the love of your life, he/she just may be waiting for you in one of the many direct sales companies out there!

- **It offers flexible work schedules.** If you have kids, then you already know how difficult it is to juggle career and family. If you do not have a family yet, then it might be a good idea to start building a legacy for them now before they show up! The stress of balancing work and raising a family usually takes a toll on many marriages. Sunny and I experienced this firsthand, and all I can say is thank God we found this industry!

- **It is a good way to earn extra income without working a second job.** I know many people who started working in their business on a part-time basis before going full-time. For 4 months, I worked part-time in my business before making the decision to go full-time when my income surpassed the money I was earning at my job.

- **It is a good way to start a business because of the turnkey system.** There are so many people out there who want to start a business but do not know how or where to begin. The beauty of network marketing for the distributor (you) is the fact that the company worries about all that goes into getting a business off the ground. For the most part, all that distributors have to do is to acquire the customers and advertise the business through word-of-mouth marketing. This makes owning your own business less capital intensive.

- **Your earnings are in proportion to the amount of effort you invest in your business.** You get to write your own paycheck in this industry. If you want to earn more than you are currently earning in your business, all you have to do is go out there and sell more products or services and advertise your business more. The level of success you can achieve is limited only by your willingness to work hard.

- **Anyone can do it.** I love this! There are no required levels of education, experience, financial resources or physical condition. People of all ages and from all backgrounds have succeeded in direct selling. I always say that everyone – including your grandmother CAN start and own a profitable direct sales business. Age is definitely nothing but a number in the direct sales industry.

- **Direct sellers are independent contractors.** You're your own boss, which means you can work part-time or full-time – you choose when and how much you want to work. Set your own goals and determine for yourself how to reach them with the help of your sponsorship line.

One of the most important benefits I've found in my business, however, is the amount of personal growth and development that occurred in every area of my life once I totally surrendered to the process.

****

"Your companies, along with millions of individual direct sellers, not only help our economy grow, but keep the American dream alive."

- U.S. Senator John McCain (R-AZ)

The first step toward success is taken when you refuse to be a captive of the environment in which you first find yourself.
~Mark Caine~

www.kingpinyin.com

"Direct selling has never gotten its due from Wall Street. It's time we recognize that the direct sales model works, and it works well."

- Jim Cramer, CNBC

Chapter 2

Why the Buzz?

It is not uncommon for people to ask network marketers why they are in one of "those things". Unfortunately, many people associate our business with illegal pyramid schemes. Even with all the success that Sunny and I have experienced over the years in the industry, people still turn up their noses at me for being in a "pyramid". It used to bother me, and I'd often find myself being sucked into a debate about the legitimacy of my business. But the more I read up about the industry from those who were top earners and other reliable sources, the easier it became for me to deal with the doubting Thomases. So do not get worked up the next time someone hits you with that infamous "is it a pyramid?" question. It may actually be a great chance to hand them a copy of this book and send them to the websites listed in Chapter 1. Knowledge rightly used is power!

Direct Selling continues to successfully deliver a strong return on investment and creates opportunities for millions of people around the world. While direct selling is best known in local communities for providing opportunities for entrepreneurs, it is also a viable, long-term investment opportunity on Wall Street. In the latest global data, most publicly traded direct selling companies reported strong earnings and income – in some cases realizing an increase of more than 250 percent in stock price from 2009 – 2011.

The direct selling industry is a growing force in the global economy and remains an attractive investment opportunity because of its long-term growth potential. The industry, over the last 150 years, has continued to grow and deliver strong return on investment. Analysts are consistent in providing positive valuations calling for long-term stock investments in publicly traded companies. Many analysts have cited the operating margins, including low overhead costs, low operating costs with minimal marketing and advertising costs, as a positive to many of these companies.

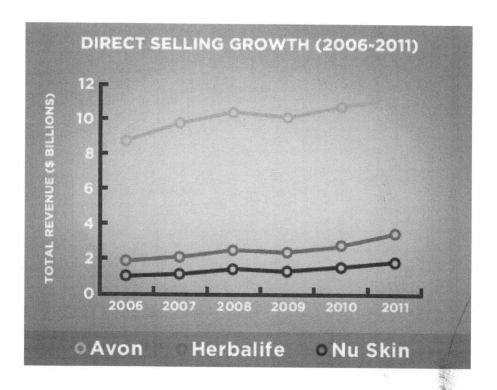

Sales in the U.S. are robust; approximately $30 billion, and sales in other countries also continue to grow. Outside the U.S., countries with the highest sales include Japan ($23.8 billion); China ($16.3 billion); Korea ($12.9 billion) and Brazil ($12.5 billion). © 2014 Direct Selling Association

Direct selling has attracted savvy investors from around the world, including billionaires like Warren Buffet (Kirby & The Pampered Chef), George Soros (Herbalife), Roger Barnett (Shaklee), Arthur L. Williams (Primerica Financial Services), Kenny A. Trout (Excel Communications), Rich DeVos (Amway), Carl Icahn (Herbalife), Donald Trump (Trump Network), Sir Richard Branson (Virgin Vie At Home) and many others whom we do not even know of. Obviously, these investors realize that network marketing done right is not a scam. Legitimate direct sellers have worked hard to clearly differentiate themselves from illegal pyramid schemes operating outside the confines of the law and the industry's self-regulatory environment. It is this differentiation that has led to the industry's increasing popularity and growing profits. In this year's 2014 Direct Selling News Global 100 list, eight companies had annual revenues above $1 Billion.

Direct Sales Pioneers

I have made it a practice to read the biographies of billionaires and have since extended that list to include network-marketing founders. Take the case of self-made billionaire Arthur (Art) L. Williams, the founder of Primerica Financial Services in 1977. Citigroup later bought the company in 1989. In 1967, Art Williams was a high school football coach in Georgia with no corporate business experience and an annual income of $10,700. Within 10 years of starting his company, A.L. Williams & Associates, he was a leader in his industry with about 180,000 people and $81 billion of individual life insurance in 1987. In his book, **All You Can Do Is All You Can Do**, Art shares the system that he used to become a billionaire and changed the lives of thousands of people in the process. According to the DSA, Primerica's 2013 revenue was $1.27 Billion!

No story about network marketing billionaires can be told without mentioning pioneers like philanthropist and NBA Orlando Magic owner Rich DeVos and his business partner Jay Van Andel. Rich helped shape the industry and founded the largest network marketing company in history – Amway – from ground up! Today Amway is one of the world's largest companies with total 2013 revenue of $11.8 Billion! I picked up a copy of his memoir **Simply Rich** and was fascinated by his rags-to-riches story and the many obstacles he had to overcome to build one of the world's largest direct sales companies.

Women were not left out of the free enterprise revolution. In 1963, Mary Kay Ash was raising three kids as a single mother. She started her company with her total life savings of $5000. Once listed among Fortune's Most Admired

Corporations in America, Mary Kay Cosmetics Inc. boasted annual 2013 revenue of $3.60 Billion! The incredible thing about these visionaries is not only the fact that they have created generational wealth for their families; but they have also given the distributors a chance to create a legacy for their families as well. In her book *Mary Kay: You Can Have It All*, this dynamic woman shares lifetime wisdom and success secrets that she used to create a multibillion-dollar international company as well as a fulfilling life that reflects her values.

Something To Think About….

Now that you know a little bit more about the network marketing industry, I must ask you one question before we get into the business of MLM.

Are you a Lion, who is hungry and fiercely chasing the freedom and abundance that we were all promised; or are you a Gazelle, running to keep your head above water, overcome fears, doubts, insecurities and struggles just so you can stay alive? Unfortunately, an overwhelming majority of the population are lions in gazelle clothing! You have been running away for so long that you've forgotten your true identity and settled for a life below what you are capable of manifesting.

I know this to be true because that was my reality prior to August 28, 2005. I woke up to the alarm clock with the rest of the world; took a 'quick' shower like the rest of the world; ate my breakfast in the car like most commuters; dealt with the rush hour traffic with the rest of the world; grumbled about it all the way to work; clocked in at 9:00 a.m. and out at 5:00 p.m. Monday through Friday with the rest of the world. I was fed up with how much I was being paid an hour, but, like the rest of the world, I settled for it anyway. I hated on the 3% that were on the golf courses, traveling the world and living the good life because I thought I could never be one of them!

Meanwhile, like clockwork, we were always broke by the 21st of the month in spite of the 4 jobs between us! Does any of this sound familiar to you? I know I was not the only one who felt this way. But, at some point in life, we've got to start asking ourselves the right questions. It sounds so easy for me to say this to you now, but I did not have the mental capacity to see that I was going about the business of life and wealth creation the wrong way back then.

My husband and I were too busy working a job and helping someone else build a legacy for the generations that followed them. It never once crossed our minds that if something were to happen to us, our jobs could not be willed to Denzel. Besides, I'm not sure he would have wanted our jobs anyway! Soccer and basketball are his current passions. Maybe like us, you have not given this any serious thought because you feel overwhelmed and helpless, or because you do not know when, where, what and how to start. The purpose of this book is to let you know that you are never without options. You have a say in how your life is unfolding. At any point in time, you can CHOOSE another option if the current one is not yielding the results you desire.

We had our rude awakening when we found out that we were having a baby in 2001! That must have been the worst day in my life because I knew that we were not ready for another mouth to feed and another soul to love. Denzel was born in July of 2002 and all hell broke loose. For about a year, we struggled to make life okay for him, but finally made the painful decision to send him home to our parents in Africa! That's when reality sank in! That's when I finally started asking the right questions. That's when it dawned on me that it was insanity to keep doing the same things and expecting a different set of results. That's when I realized it was time to make a shift from my gazelle mode into lion mode. They say nothing can stop a mind that is made up and it is so true. Especially when desperation kicks in.

Making The Shift

The quickest way to turn your life around is to start asking yourself some hard questions. The truth began to emerge when I started asking the right questions. These statistics will blow your mind. So let me share them with you here.

- The average American life span is about 81 years for women and 77 years for men.

- Americans will spend one third of their life span working a job.

- You will spend approximately 2100 hours on your job this year.

- A 40 year career span = 84,000 hours on a job you don't like!!!!

Reality Check

- You spend about 10 hours/day at your job.

- You spend about 8 hours/day sleeping.

- You spend about 4 hours/day on household activities, leisure and sports.

- *You only have 2 hour/day for your personal growth & development and to start a new business!*

Now you understand why change is difficult to achieve for the majority of the population. It is because it takes time, the luxury of which most of us do not have. But here's the good news: now that you are aware of the things that are competing for your time, you can set reasonable timeframes for yourself. It took my husband and I a total of nine months to make the transition from working a job into entrepreneurship. Then it took us another three years to fully settle into business ownership. It was the craziest time in our lives because a lot of things had to shift in order for us to accomplish our dreams. But if we could put aside the social animal activities for a few months in order to create the life we now live, then so can you. You just have to decide today that enough is enough and that it's time to start living life on your terms!

Real Talk

According to my research from Career Builder and Gallop Poll surveys:

- 70% of people DO NOT like their jobs.

- 50% of people DO NOT feel fulfilled.

- 20% of employees know that their job is the #1 cause of stress in their lives. Hence they are actively disengaged from the workplace.

- 43% of the working class lives paycheck to pay check.

- 27% of people DO NOT save any money from their paycheck.

- 37% of people manage to save $250 or less.

- 10% of people can afford to save $1000 or more.

- 67% of the population is working in the wrong field.

- 72% of employees are in a job where they are undermined and passed over for promotion regularly either because of race, gender, educational background etc.

- 50% of employees work while on vacation.

I'm sure you're beginning to see the big picture already. It is very important to note here that not everybody is interested in living in abundance. Some people are okay with the status quo. The information that I am sharing with you in this book is for those who want more out of life.

This information is for those who, like me, believe that they can be, do and have more in every area of their lives. You'll know if you are one of those people because several light bulbs will go off for you as you read through the pages of this book.

I believe that the direct sales industry provides a way out of the rat race for those who are very serious about wanting more.

If you doubt it, take a look at the chart below and then decide for yourself.

Total Global Sales for 2012

INDUSTRY	SALES
The NFL	$10 Billion
Music Industry	$17 Billion
Video Gaming	$67 Billion
Movies Industry	$80 Billion
Organic Products	$91 Billion
Direct Sales	$178 Billion

How about that for size? The above chart simply shows you that the chances of succeeding are a lot higher in the direct sales industry than in these industries, and the playing field is more even.

****

"Direct selling is a great model... with high gross margins, low capital intensity, lots of free cash flow... It's a fragmented industry with gigantic room for growth... the top 15 players only account for about half the market."

- Jim Cramer, CNBC

"You offer us a chance to send a very different message. It's not just a message of go find a job, it's a message of create your own job, while being your own boss by participating in a system of free enterprise where you can in fact create a better future."

— Former Speaker of the House, Newt Gingrich (R-GA)

Chapter 3

Choosing The Right Company

I am investing a great deal of time in Part I of this book to help you make an informed decision about starting a home-based business. Worth mentioning here is the difference between a legitimate MLM, direct sales, or network marketing company and a pyramid scheme. You will be surprised at how many of our friends and family members have had the misfortune of entering into illegal pyramids that were disguised as network marketing or direct sales companies.

As you read through the definitions, you'll see clearly that the main distinction is between the sale of products and services versus enrolling representatives into the company. The Direct Selling Association (DSA) and its sister companies have fought long and hard to differentiate between legitimate multilevel direct selling companies and illegal pyramid promotional schemes.

The U.S. Federal Trade Commission (FTC) has regulatory authority over many U.S. business activities, including direct selling. That authority has been used to set anti-pyramid standards and has been instrumental in determining the business standards used by legitimate multilevel companies in the United States.

What is Direct Selling?

According to www.directselling.com, direct selling is *the sale of a consumer product or service*, person-to-person, away from a fixed retail location, marketed through independent sales representatives who are sometimes also referred to as consultants, distributors or other titles. Just about any product or service can be purchased through direct selling somewhere in the world. Many people think of cosmetics, wellness products and home décor as products that are often sold through direct sales, but add to that countless other product categories including kitchen products, jewelry, clothing, organic gardening supplies, spa products, scrapbooking supplies, rubber stamps and much, much more. (http://www.directselling411.com).

The products and services sold by legitimate multilevel marketing and direct selling companies are in fact used or consumed, and the compensation is based upon those sales for consumption by the end-users.

What is an Illegal Pyramid Scheme?

In a pyramid scheme, the products or services — if any do actually exist — are not used or consumed by anyone. Instead, money is made from the mere act of recruiting new participants into the scheme.

The old adage is true: There is no such thing as getting something for nothing!

If it sounds too good to be true, then it probably is. The Federal Trade Commission's (FTC) test for determining whether a disguised network marketing company or multilevel marketing (MLM) business is a pyramid scheme reads as follows: a pyramid scheme is *"characterized by the payment by participants of money to the company in return for which they (1) receive the right to sell a product and (2) the right to receive in return for recruiting other participants into the program rewards which are unrelated to sale of the product to ultimate users."*

(http://www.ftc.gov/system/files/documents/cases/140605burnloungeopinion.pdf)

Not all MLM businesses are illegal pyramid schemes. To determine whether an MLM business is a pyramid, a court must look at how the MLM business operates in practice. Unfortunately, because many people get sucked into the idea of becoming a millionaire overnight, these pyramid schemes are always going to prey on the naivety of many uninformed individuals.

A few years ago, the gifting circle pyramid scheme made its rounds across the country. I received a call from a friend who was working the business with me at the time. She sounded incredibly excited about a new business venture that was going to make us rich without the 'hard work' we were currently investing into our MLM business.

All we had to do was invest $5000 and then look for eight women who wanted to 'gift' a poor widow in a third world country with the same amount in order to earn $40,000. I asked her what products and services we would be selling in return and her response was 'nothing'! I happened to have been driving back home from a business road trip that had taken me to DE, NJ, NY, MA, NH, and I had to pull over to be sure that I heard her very well.

It took me a good 45mins in vain trying to talk her out of losing $5000! I had done my homework about the difference between network marketing and pyramid schemes. She had not.

Needless to say that when the scheme was finally exposed, there were many angry hopeful millionaires walking around. The only ones who end up with millions of dollars are the con artists who put together these schemes.

One of the best write ups that I have read about this is a 5 pages document titled: *Legitimate Direct Selling vs. Illegal Pyramid Schemes, A White Paper by Amy Robinson.* You can find it here: http://www.dsa.org/docs/default-source/direct-selling-facts/internalconsumptionwhitepaper.pdf?sfvrsn=2.

I have included a few key points from that white paper below to give you an idea of what to look out for.

Examples of protections included in DSA's Code of Ethics:

Inventory Buyback – In addition, Direct Selling Association member companies pledge to repurchase inventory from any salesperson that decides to leave the business. Any inventory purchased in the year prior to a salesperson's departure is repurchased for at least 90 percent of what was originally paid. Thus, the proverbial problem of "inventory loading" – a garage full of inventory that no one can sell – and the resultant loss of thousands of dollars is eliminated.

No Large Up-Front Fees – DSA members have also pledged not to charge unreasonable, large up-front fees to become a direct seller.

No "Headhunting Fees" – DSA members have also pledged not to make payments for recruiting an individual a primary part of their compensation plans. Instead, DSA members pay for the sale of real product to real users – not for recruitment.

No Outrageous, Unsubstantiated Earnings Claims – DSA members pledge not to make claims that salespeople can make large amounts of money without time, commitment and effort, and any earnings claims that are made must be based on documented evidence and a real track record.

Other industry practices to which the FTC has pointed as evidence that compensation is based on sales, not recruitment:

A Minimum Customer Rule – Many direct selling companies have adopted some version of the company policy the FTC found helpful in the Amway case. It provided that in order to receive compensation a certain number (ten in that case) of sales to customers had to be demonstrated in any month. Again, these are merely self-imposed company policies.

A 70% Rule – Similarly, although not required by law or regulation, many companies have adopted a policy similar to one of Amway's internal policies rules. That protection provided that "every distributor must sell at wholesale and/or retail at least 70% of the inventory he bought during a given month in order to receive [compensation]…"

What to look for in a company - This brings us to the topic of how to choose the best company for you. We have been incredibly blessed and fortunate to be with one company for nine years! Not everybody can say that in an industry like ours. This does not mean that there is anything wrong with those true leaders who have been in more than one opportunity. Some people have been forced to move because the company went under or was shut down by the attorney general for non-compliance.

Do your due diligence - A legitimate opportunity will not disappear overnight.

Think long-term when making the decision to start with a company. This is one sure way of avoiding the pyramid scheme trap.

I think that many people make an emotional decision when it comes to starting a business in direct sales because of the personal relationship they have with the person who introduced them to the business. The bad guys know this too! That's why it's so easy for these schemes to be disguised as direct sales companies. Due diligence can also be the reason why you miss out on an opportunity because you talked to the ones who did not succeed. This is the equivalence of asking a doctor's opinion about becoming an engineer! Or like asking me what I think about you becoming an astronaut!

Choose a company whose products and services appeal to you. - It will be almost impossible for you to market a product that you do not believe in yourself. Remember that the real money in network marketing is in the products and services portfolio. If you cannot get excited about the products in a company's portfolio, it will be very difficult for you to represent them.

Ask questions - Ask about the company, the management team, its field leadership, the products or services, the compensation plan structure, start-up fees, realistic costs of doing business, average earnings of distributors, return policies, and anything else you're concerned about. Don't wait to go home and ask your family members and friends who were not at the opportunity meeting. Ask the experts and they'll have the correct answers to help you make an informed decision.

Get copies of all company literature - Visit the company's website. Ask for additional literature from the person who referred you to the company and read it! Many people miss out because of lack of knowledge.

Consult with others who have had experiences with the company and its products - Check to see if the products or services are actually being sold to consumers. It's very easy to verify these days through social media. It's hard to miss on Facebook and Instagram if the distributors love the products and whether they are getting results from using them. That's all they will talk about. You can also easily find out if they are successful with the business venture on social media! God bless Instagram and Facebook!

Fast Facts

According to the website www.directselling411.com:

- **76%** of sellers have been with their company 1+ years

- **78%** of sellers say direct selling meets or exceeds their expectations

- **82%** of sellers report a good, very good or excellent experience with direct selling

- **74%** of US adults have purchased products from a direct seller

- **15.9 million** people in the U.S. are involved in direct selling

- **$31.63 billion** in total US sales

- **$166.9 billion** sales worldwide

I truly believe that we were born to be great, and to have the things that make us happy. Hence we are only as limited as our thinking. It's time to ignite our lives.

www.kingpinyin.com

As part of the direct selling industry, you each know firsthand the value of opportunity within the free enterprise system. Your participation in the direct selling industry has also contributed significantly to the economic growth our nation has experienced in recent years."

- U.S. Representative Pete Sessions (R-TX)

Chapter 4

Understanding The Importance Of Using Systems In Direct Sales

The best definition of the word system that I have heard so far is **S**ave **Y**ourself **S**tress **T**ime **E**nergy & **M**oney! That's exactly what every successful company in the world has done. They have put systems in place for their routine activities. The best way for me to explain why having a system is so important to your business is to use the example of a company that we are all very familiar with – Wal-Mart.

Since Sam Walton opened his first discount store in Rogers, Arkansas, in 1962, they have built hundreds across the U.S. Wal-Mart operates nearly **11,000 retail units** under 71 banners in **27 countries** and e-commerce websites in **10 countries**. They employ **2.2 million associates** around the world — **1.3 million in the U.S.** alone. How did Mr. Sam (as he is fondly called) accomplish this gigantic feat? By using a system in his business operations!

What is a System?

The website www.businessdictionary.com defines a system in two ways. First, as a set of detailed methods, procedures and routines created to carry out a specific activity, perform a duty, or solve a problem. And secondly as an organized, purposeful structure that consists of interrelated and interdependent elements (components, entities, factors, members, parts etc.). These elements continually influence one another (directly or indirectly) to maintain their activity and the existence of the system, in order to achieve the goal of the system.

If we go by the above definitions, Wal-Mart is one of the world's most successful retailers, managing about $32 billion of inventory because the organization invested the time and money in order to create one of the best supply chain management systems. Regardless of where the Wal-Mart store operates — Bentonville, AK, Baltimore, MD, or Leeds, England — the processes and the systems are generally the same. Wal-Mart is able to transfer people from one store to the other, and they're able to pick up right where the previous employee left off, resulting in significantly less downtime or startup time in the transition. Very few companies can boast of a centralized system of operations like that.

The great thing about our industry is the fact that most companies have already invested the time and money to create a system that works for its distributors. I strongly recommend that you stick with your company's system if you want to succeed. If your company does not have a clear-cut system in place, then look to your upline leadership for the system they have created to help you grow your downline and customer base. Think of a system as your roadmap to the top of your compensation plan! I will go into greater details about business building activities in Part II of this book, but a great system should cover everything, including the following:

- **How to talk to prospects**. Generic scripts for acquiring customers and for recruiting new business partners into the business. There is a right and wrong way to present your business and its portfolio. Hence the need for a generic script to aid and guide new distributors.

Many direct sales careers have been aborted at this stage! Ignorance on fire without a system to follow can be very dangerous. Looking back, there were many times in the early days when I had NO clue how to approach a prospect because I did not follow the system. I shudder at my approach today!

- **Where to find these prospects**. We call this in my company the *Memory Jogger* list. You will be surprised how quickly distributors can exhaust their warm market (family and friends). A memory jogger will remind them of all the potential prospects they interact with during the course of their day.

- **The enrollment process**. Enrolling a new distributor into the business and the action steps they need to take immediately to get their business off to a great start. This is a very important step in the system. I know the excitement of signing up new partners into your business, but you do not want to be a leader who does this yourself.

I had a leader in my organization that would collect all the new representative agreements after a business presentation and take them home with her to personally enroll these folks into the business! Needless to say, this became very cumbersome and time consuming for her when the business reached the momentum phase.

- **How to use their personal website to order products and services**. This is another very important step in the process. Our business thrives on a large customer base.

- **How to use their virtual office and where to find the most important documents in their back office.**

- **How to prepare for and set up their first home meeting and subsequent meetings**. Include a list of what is acceptable behavior before, during and after the private meeting. Make sure that they have a DVD player and a remote control that actually works! You'd be surprised at how many technical difficulties we have experienced because the DVD player or the remote control did not work like it should!

- **How to setup and run effective weekly formal business opportunity meetings**. You want to streamline this process so that like Wal-Mart, your weekly opportunity meeting format across the country are the same. A new guest should see the same presentation slide and receive the same information in Atlanta, GA as they would in Los Angeles, CA. This is extremely important in order for massive duplication to occur.

- The personal marketing materials needed. Explain to them why they need to have company opportunity and product brochures, DVDs, magazines, business cards etc.

If you want to go fast in network marketing, go alone. But if you want to go far, go with a team of people. However, do not take this to mean that I'm encouraging you to babysit your business partners. The core of our business model is centered on being able to duplicate yourself. The only way to successfully do that is to create a system that works and insist that the system be duplicated across your entire organization. The new representatives will not understand this initially, but they will later on, and they will thank you for insisting that they save themselves stress, time and money by sticking with the system.

Understanding the Purpose of the Quick Start Process:

• Provides a simple, well-planned, easy-to-follow **system** with a clear road map to successfully build the business.

- Helps you experience early success that will keep you motivated and fired up.

- Guarantees long-term retention in your business. The first 90 days are critical to the life span of your business.

- Helps you qualify for the initial bonuses.

- Helps with the goals setting process.

- Every new representative deserves to be pointed towards the right direction. Failure to follow the quick start process sets them up for failure as they do not get 100% of the knowledge needed to build a successful business.

- Without a system in place, information will be lost through generations of your business as your organization grows larger.

- Mastery of this process will result in **massive duplication** throughout the organization.

Part II

Business Building Activities

There are 8760 hours in a year. You have the power to transform your life if you invest just one of those hours each week to think about your life's purpose.

"Direct selling has never gotten its due from Wall Street. It's time we recognize that the direct sales model works, and it works well."

— Jim Cramer, CNBC

Chapter 5

The Recruiting Process

The recruiting process is the lifeline of your new business! However, the very idea of recruiting new people into the business is extremely painful for a vast majority of new and old distributors alike. I believe that the reason for this is because many of us were taught, as children, not to speak to strangers.

Now that we are adults and are no longer vulnerable, no one has told us that it is okay to talk to and make new friends by talking to strangers. If you just had a light bulb go off, then this will be a good time to take a few minutes off, close your eyes, take a deep breath and try to override the old programming that says strangers are evil and must be avoided.

Replace that thought pattern with the fact that it's okay to talk to strangers because that's how you make new friends and grow your business. Feel free to perform this little exercise over and over again until the message reaches your subconscious mind.

The recruiting process is simply the series of activities that occur after you join a company and create your prospect list. It is what you do next to create a method out of the myriad of "to dos" on your list.

The good news is that if you are working with a progressive group, then the leader would have already created a simple and effective process for the team to follow. Otherwise, you might waste a lot of precious time trying to make sense out of the madness of starting a new business and time wasted is money.

Do not be fooled by the simplicity of the process created by your company or leaders. I have seen many new distributors fail because they tried to over complicate the process. Your leaders got to their position in the company by following the system that they are trying to teach you. The process generally includes activities like cold and warm market prospecting, effective follow-ups, private business receptions (PBR), weekly opportunity briefings and using the power of the Internet to grow your business in this day and age.

The idea is to keep it simple so that everyone in your business can duplicate the process without you. The average person will not be able to follow the process if it's too complicated. One important thing for you to know before setting off on this process is how much time you have available to grow your business.

Setting Attainable Goals:

How much time are you willing to invest into your business? You have to know how much time you have available to work your business in order for you to set realistic goals. A typical organization will have busy professionals like doctors, lawyers, accountants, and others who will be pressed for time. It will be a little bit unreasonable to have the same time and commitment expectations from these people like you would for a stay-at-home mom. The table below will help guide your business and recruiting goals as it will reveal how much time you have at your disposal to build the business.

We all have 24 hours a day and 7 days in a week, which equal 168 hours in total. I've included some basic activities that a majority of people perform on a daily basis. Fill in the number of hours you spend at your job, on meals, taking bathroom breaks, etc. How many days per week do you perform these activities? Multiply these numbers and fill in the total number of hours in the total column.

For example, if you work 8hrs/day, five days a week, the total number of hours you spend at your job a week is 40 hours. Do the same for all the rows and then subtract the Total column from 168 hours (the number of hours available a week). The result will be the number of hours you have to invest into your business and personal development.

❖ **7 days X 24 hours/day = 168 hours per week!**

ACTIVITY	HOURS/DAY	DAYS/WEEK	TOTAL
Job			
Meals			
Bathroom Breaks			
Family			
Recreation			
Sleep			
Total Hours Used up per week			
Available Hours			

Use your available hours to set realistic goals for your business in order to avoid undue stress.

Creating a List

- The recruiting process begins with your list. A phone contact sheet is not a list! Write the names down on paper. A piece of paper is not a list either. Invest in a journal or notebook so that you can keep track of your daily activities as you begin to call these prospects.

- Create a name and comment column in the journal or notepad. It is very good practice to give yourself feedback on how the call went. Did they ask you to callback? If so, when? What time? Etc.

- Schedule a time to actually call these prospects. Many people will create a list and never schedule time to call the people on the list. There's a lot competing with your time and if you do not carve out time to call these people, you'll never grow your business and reach your goals. Whatever gets scheduled gets done!

- Check with your leaders about what resources and tools to use for this process. Your company's "quick start" or getting started document in your virtual office should have this information as well.

- Practice reading, out loud, the sample scripts provided by your company before you begin making actual calls.

List Sorting Process

- You are now ready to go about your business, and your number one goal is to arouse the curiosity of the people on your list enough for them to want more.

-If you filled out the table above, you now know how much time you have daily to make your calls. One to two hours a day is great since you'll be spending less than 10 minutes per call.

- Start working that phone with a big smile on your face! Play catch up with your prospect first before talking about the business. The perfect time to talk about the reason for your call is when they ask after you. Use the script, send them a link, or a third party tool like a DVD, CD, website, magazine, etc. and schedule a follow-up call within 48 hours if they agree to look to review the resources.

- Remember that "less is more" during this phase of the recruiting process. Do not be sucked into answering questions about the business since you are still very new to the company. Leave the explanations to your leaders and the company tools like pique calls, a link to a pique video, brochures and magazines. If they insist, politely let them know that the tool you are pointing them to will do a better job explaining the opportunity to them than you can ever do. Reassure them that you'll put them in touch with an expansion leader once they review the resource. This will also be a great time to edify the leader in case they want to speak or meet with the leader if he or she is local.

- Do not stop until you are done calling every prospect on your list for the day. Many people will stop after the first call because they did not get a yes! Remember, all you are doing is sorting for the few who are interested in knowing why you are so excited! Do not become attached to the outcome. Just keep sorting.

Expert Calls

The purpose of this step is to have an expansion leader in your business to talk briefly with your prospect on a 3-way call. This should only happen after they have listened to, watched or reviewed the pique resource tool that you shared with them in Step One above and have some questions about what they reviewed. You must have someone at a higher pin level working with you since it is almost impossible for you to move your friends and family to the next step in the recruiting process by yourself. The right format to follow is to call the prospect first and then get your leader on a 3-way call to talk with your prospect. Their goal will not only be to answer any questions that your prospect may have, but also to invite them to your grand opening reception. In order for the leader to get your prospect to come out to your grand opening, you must properly edify the leader. It is very important that you learn how to correctly edify your leadership.

Scheduling your Grand Opening (PBR)

This is your **private business reception (PBR)**. Every new company has a grand opening and yours should be no different. The majority of people you know will prefer to come to your house for a business reception than come out to a formal hotel presentation. Check with your leaders and schedule it within 7-10 days of signing up. If you want to grow a large organization in network marketing, make home meetings and private business receptions the lifeblood of your business. I encourage you to schedule at least 3 or more home parties in your first month. This will get your business off the ground quickly and introduce the new venture to your friends and family in the comfort of your home. Those who see an opportunity for themselves will join you on the journey and those who do not will end up being your customers if they like your products. They will also send you referrals if you ask them to support you in that way.

Those who make PBRs/home parties a routine activity will set the right precedence in their group and they will consistently outperform anyone who is not hosting regular home meetings. Reason being that home parties create momentum for your business. People do what people see. Your new business partners will assume that they have to host daily or weekly PBRs if they see you doing the same when they start. How you start with them is how they will start their new partners. In a nutshell, this process is: creating a list, piquing their interest with tools, passing them to your leader, hosting a home party or PBR, signing them up and repeating the process.

In some cases, you may have to invite them out to a formal business presentation to see the bigger vision before they'll sign up. In that case, the expansion leader will extend the invitation at the end of the grand opening and your job will be to follow up with them during the week before the day of the meeting. We'll talk more about the importance of weekly briefings in the Events chapter.

Prospecting to Grow Your Team

What happens when a new distributor runs out of people to talk to in their immediate circle?

Besides your warm market, (friends and family), you should pique peoples' interest as you go about your daily activities. I believe that your warm market is a great place for you to start so that you can get the rejections and emotions out of building the business. Initially, I had an incredibly rough time with my immediate circle. It took me four months to get the ones with influence to see my new business as a viable business venture. Family can be disappointing sometimes only because they know you too well —or they think they do! Once I got past the pain of their doubts and rejection, I was able to prospect outside of my warm market much more easily. The main thing is to remember that when someone says 'no' to you, it has absolutely nothing to do with you! It just might not be the right time or vehicle for them. Do not take it personally.

If you leave home daily, you're walking past prospects every day. There is a right and wrong way to approach someone you do not know about a business opportunity. Make sure that you look successful and well groomed. You may be wondering, "What does this have to do with anything?" The answer is EVERYTHING! I made the mistake of buying into the idea that 'it's about the message and not the messenger' in the beginning of my career. Boy, was I wrong!

People will judge you based on your looks 90% of the time. They'll see you before they hear what you have to say. So, the first few seconds are crucial and looking the part of a successful entrepreneur will go a very long way when you are out prospecting total strangers. Your clothes should be clean and pressed. Your manicure should be new and elegant, not chipped. No claws please! Your shoes should be polished. Your hair should be properly cut or styled for ladies. Please use deodorant, cologne, perfume and breath mints. You are the message and the messenger.

The next thing you should know is that you must look like you are having a lot of fun doing what you do. If you do not exude passion and excitement, why in the world would anyone want to partner up with you? People's jobs and their lives are already boring enough! No one needs an extra source of frustration. Smile as you approach the prospect!

You must have professional third party tools from your company when you go out to prospect. Have your business cards, brochures, magazine, DVDs and

CDs handy and neatly organized in a laptop bag or briefcase. You don't want to come across as an amateur who's just out to hunt somebody down. Hunters do not eat in direct sales! Make sure that all your resources are neatly labeled with your name, email address, website and a working phone number. Remember that you are not out to do a presentation, but to pique interest, hand them a third party resource tool and ask them to call or email you if they see value in your opportunity. Do not attach yourself to the outcome. You will have to pique the interest of a lot of people to get just one person to respond. The general rule is to expect less than 1% success ratio with the cold market. But that largely depends on your prospecting technique!

Prospecting Technique

How do you break the ice when you meet a total stranger? The secret is to connect with them through a heartfelt smile. People will always smile back at you for the most part.

Then proceed to introduce yourself while extending your hand. Hi, my name is Jane. The natural response will be for them to tell you their name. Say something if their name strikes a chord with you! Like, "John? That's my dad's name!"

What you're doing is connecting by finding a common ground. Now that you have them talking, the next step is to deepen the connection using this simple **FORM** method:

> **F** - **Family**. Their family situation. Married? Kids? How many? Boy? Girl? Age group? Etc.
>
> **O** - **Occupation**. What they do for a living?
>
> **R** - **Recreation**. What they like to do for fun?
>
> **M** - **Money.** Tell them about your business!

The whole idea here is to listen to them as you lead them on. It has to be a natural process and not forced. You may not have to go through the entire acronym before they reciprocate by asking you what you do for a living! BINGO!!!!

"I live for a living!"

"What do you mean, 'you live for living?'"

"I help people to unlock their passion and live life on their terms, with no financial limits!"

What do you think will happen after this point? You guessed right! They will probably say, "Tell me more about that!"

Then you hand them your resource tool with NO strings attached. It's really that simple.

Remember to take their information, too. Now you'll be more memorable when you call them. The general rule is to call in about 48 hours — if they have not called you back already. Move them through your prospecting system from here.

That's how you keep your prospecting funnel or pipeline flowing!

Besides a *weak desire* or reason for doing the business, not having a good prospecting system to follow is the Number 1 reason why many people quit the business. For those of you who have been in the industry much longer, I hope that the content presented in this chapter, even though somewhat familiar, will motivate you to pick yourself up and start off where you left off. Reach deep within yourself and find that special something that was once the compelling reason why direct sales/MLM made so much sense for you to use as a vehicle to pursue your dreams. Re-connect with it, and let's make another run to the top of your compensation plan.

For those of you who are new to the industry, I hope this offers a crystal clear picture of what is required of you to build a successful business and establish a solid foundation from which your future organizations will take root and grow exponentially all over the world. It will be my utmost pleasure to see you grow through your company structure and become the person you have always wanted to be. Have faith and believe in yourself, for within you lies every path you can ever dream of taking and everything you dream of becoming.

Make no mistake about it; this business will require that you make significant sacrifices as you learn and advance your way to the top of your business empire. You will have some good days and some not-so-great days, but is that not what this journey called life is all about? The choices you make on any one of those 'bad' days will determine how far you go with your opportunity in network marketing. In the end, everything ultimately depends on YOU! However, remember that you will not be in business by yourself. Your company and line of sponsorship will be there to offer you valuable training and support.

Memory Jogger Acronym

> **F-** Friends

> **R-** Relatives

> **A- Acquaintances**

> **N-** Neighbors

> **K-** Kids

Creating a Compelling Vision for Your Business---Why are you in the business?

You may have heard this question countless times from your leadership, but may not have understood why it is so important. Creating a compelling vision to guide your success is critical in this business. Failure to do so will inevitably lead to failure in direct sales. What happens when you leave your home without any destination in mind? You almost certainly will end up nowhere!

In the same way, not having a clear picture of what you want to achieve, using network marketing as a vehicle, will ultimately lead you down the path to nowhere. If you fail to plan, you plan to fail!

Many distributors only have a vague idea of why they are in the business. The most basic response from business partners is usually more money; be their own bosses, etc. Even though these are great reasons, they still do not identify the tangible reasons why you are in the business. You need to find that central, significant reason for devoting your time, money, effort, energy and talent into building your business.

Finding your why is not a difficult task if you have a general idea why you are in business. Wanting to earn more money is okay, but knowing the reason behind wanting to earn more money is the compelling reason. **You should be able to list a couple of specific life changes, with details that will occur once you become successful with your business.**

For example, 'once I become successful with -------- I will buy a gorgeous house in Potomac, Maryland, with a driveway, a swimming pool, a basketball court, and a lawn tennis court.'

➢ **It is imperative that you write down these thoughts and read them aloud daily!**

➢ **Attach pictures that represent your vision.**

➢ **Make your 'why' larger than just you.**

➢ **See It in Your Mind, Feel It in Your Body, and Believe that You Will Achieve It.**

Desire is one of the strongest human forces. How badly do you want it?

www.kingpinyin.com

*"Words have incredible power. They can make people's hearts soar,
or they can make people's hearts sore."*

- Dr. Mardy Grothe

Chapter 6

How To Become A Master Presenter

Becoming an exceptional presenter is a Herculean task for most people. Sweaty palms, shaking hands, dry mouth, wobbly knees, thundering heartbeat, sudden episode of Alzheimer's, feeling faint, uncontrolled bladder, tight stomach, tied tongue and the list goes on and on! There is too much stuff to remember. Say this. Speak up. Look at the audience. Don't fidget, stand tall!

The fear of public speaking is the #1 fear in the world today! Most people would rather be in the casket at a funeral than be the one giving the eulogy! Whereas many people do not have to give a presentation by the nature of their jobs, you, however, will be required to present your business opportunity and/or your product portfolio on a daily or weekly basis. You may be able to get away without presenting the business initially, but you'll still be required to do so eventually. Once you become comfortable with this fact, the ideas I'm going to present in this chapter will help you a great deal.

Benefits of Effective Presentations

Despite all these concerns, there are several advantages to learning how to present effectively:

- **An increase in your earning potential**. Your check will go up the day you decide to stand up! Delivering effective presentations is a moneymaking activity in network marketing because the business involves showing the plan, explaining the features and benefits of your product portfolio and training your new business partners. And if you do it right, you might end up giving speeches across the country!

- **Builds credibility within your organization.** Even if your entire system is automated, leaders are still required to give presentations. One of the fastest ways to build credibility in the organization and among your peers is to give effective presentations.

- **Projects the image and presence of an inspiring leader.** Always keep in mind the fact that people are looking for someone to follow and the people in your organization are no different. They'll see in you the image and posture of that "someone" they are aspiring to be like every time you stand in front of the room giving a presentation or a speech.

- **Increases your ability to influence & lead others.** Pastor Joel Osteen, Bishop TD Jakes, Pastor Paula White, Dr Mike Murdock and several religious leaders come to mind when you talk about the ability to lead and influence people. I'm sure that there are several ministers of the gospel out there who are great speakers. The reason why they stand out is because they deliver very effective presentations every time they mount the pulpit or speak to an audience.

- **Makes a strong first impression.** The first time that we all took note of president Barack Obama was when he gave the keynote speech at the 2004 Democratic National Convention. I specifically remember thinking to myself "who is that man?" He made a very strong first impression on me and the American public; strong enough that he ran for the office of the president of the United States three years later and won it — largely due to his ability to deliver effective speeches. In the same manner, the new distributors joining your organization will form their first impression about you as their leader beginning with your presentation abilities. The good news for many people in network marketing is that you do not have to be seen as the 'leader' until you attain a certain rank in your compensation structure, and this usually takes a year or two. So, in the meantime, keep on working on your presentation skills.

- **Fast track your business**. As I mentioned before, your check will go up when you decide to take ownership of your business by improving your presentation skills. Your upline leaders will assist you with doing presentations in the beginning, but they are not going to keep doing it for you a year into the business. Besides, you really do not want to give anybody that much control over your business growth.

Start from somewhere and work towards doing your own presentations. Everyone starts off really bad before they become great. The first presentation I gave was horrible! I had a cheat sheet with me and was sweating everywhere possible! But guess what? I stood up and gave a second presentation and a third, and here we are today. You don't have to be a master presenter to start, but you have to start before you can become a master presenter.

Effective Presentations

You want to work toward becoming an effective presenter of your business opportunity and product portfolio. Presenters and presentation styles vary greatly. Everyone is unique in his or her delivery of the same content.

One of the worst mistakes you can ever make in this area is to try to be someone you're not. You need to find your flow and then develop it to the highest level possible.

A great place to start is to ask yourself these questions:

-What makes a presenter exceptional?

-What moves you when you listen to a presentation?

Exceptional presentations are a combination of many things. Before we go into how to give great presentations, take time to think about and answer the following questions.

Write down the names of at least 3 exceptional presenters in your company or otherwise:

_____

_____

_____

What makes each of them to stand out?

_____

_____

_____

List 5 characteristics or traits for each of them:

_____

_____

_____

Most human beings learn through observation. That's why people do what you do and not what you say. I prefer for you to start developing your personal skills by observing the leaders in your company. You will be required to give the exact presentation that they are currently doing on your behalf in the near future. Once you become comfortable with that, broaden your sphere by observing other effective presenters in the public speaking industry, on television, political arena, religious world, etc.

Rating yourself as a presenter

Before you start working on the process of improving upon yourself, you must first take stock of what you are currently working with. Remember that the whole purpose of this chapter is to make you a better leader. Please be honest with yourself because no one is going to see or grade your responses.

Using a scale of 1-10 (10 being the best):

What are your greatest strengths as a presenter?

_____

_____

_____

What are your areas of greatest need & refinement?

_____

_____

_____

Are you comfortable presenting to people you know or people you don't know? What is the difference?

_____

_____

_____

What impression do you make on your audience?

_____

_____

_____

Have you used videotaping to critic yourself before? What did you learn?

_____

_____

_____

Something to think about:
How do you know if your presentation skills are lacking? Do you have a coach?

_____

_____

_____

Most people do not like being the bearer of bad news. There's something about our culture that does not like hurting people's feelings. Most people do not gracefully accept criticism either. But I believe that a dose of reality can serve as a wakeup call and encourage us to improve on our presentation skills. You probably will never hear anyone say something like:

-"Lucy, your speech was horrible! I am sure you did not spend enough time to prepare for it!"

-"Sunny, we appreciate your coming in and boring us to death this afternoon!"

-"King, of all the speakers at this conference today, you were, without question, the worst!"

The only people in your company who can effectively critic your presentation skills are the people in your business who are exceptional presenters themselves. And in most cases, they will be generous with their critic.

I believe that the best way to develop your presentation skills is to have a coach. They'll be able to give you a more objective feedback on what you need to improve upon, remove from or add to your presentation skill. It will be well worth the investment. My presentation skills dramatically improved only after I started paying top dollars for coaching and mentoring from industry experts.

1. Secrets of the Master Presenters:

- **Be Organized.**

Master presenters take charge of the presentation process from start to finish. They understand that it is a process and everything counts starting with their appearance. People will generally judge you based on what they see before they hear you. Master presenters look poised and polished. They are well groomed. They spend enough time researching their presentation topic and because of this they sound prepared when they deliver the presentation. When you listen to someone who has done their homework on their presentation topic, you get the sense that they are not there to waste your time. Their message is well structured and clearly defined, usually starting with an opening, followed by a body and a close.

- *Opening:* **introduce yourself and tell them what you are going to tell them**
- **Body: present the content of your information providing advantages and benefits.**
- *Close:* **summary of what you just told them and close with a call to action.**
- **The Four Components of any Presentation**

Let's go deeper with the previous information. You must pay attention to details if you want to be seen as an organized master presenter.

A. Purpose/Mission/Goal: Put yourself in the position of your audience by asking yourself these questions:

- **Why are we here?**
- **Why did your audience leave everything to come listen to your business opportunity presentation?**

Giving a presentation without knowing the purpose is like taking a journey without knowing your destination. I'm sure you have heard your leaders say that if you fail to plan you plan to fail. This applies when you prepare for your presentation as well. If you clearly define your purpose for giving the presentation, you will find it easier to keep your information relevant.

Set the stage for your presentation content by telling them what you want them to remember the most when they leave the business opportunity presentation. For example, "If you remember one thing when you leave here today, I want you to remember this..."

B. Current Situation/Issues:

Now that your audience knows what to expect, here's your chance to tell them what you really want to tell them about your magnificent business opportunity and your product portfolio. What is going on that you want them to know about so that they can make an informed decision? How are things positioned with your company? What is the trend? How does your company address the issue? If you are in a company that offers health and nutritional products for instance, then you'll want to update them about the health statistics in your country and make it real to them as you talk about your products.

Example: *Obesity is common, serious and costly and more than one-third of U.S. adults (34.9%) are obese, according to the Journal of American Medicine (JAMA).*

Using third party sources adds credibility to your business opportunity and to your presentation.

C. Benefits/Outcome/Consequences:

If you do an outstanding job explaining the current situation and issues, then you should already have the audience nodding and agreeing with you on a number of things. Now is the time to tell them about what's in it for them by showing them your compensation plan structure. Remember to stress the benefits of your opportunity and product portfolio. I usually think about the advantages, disadvantages, consequences and implications of taking or not taking action as I go through the compensation plan. If your company offers residual income versus linear income, this will be the time to stress the importance of working hard and smart for a few years so that you can either work part-time after that or retire and live on your residual income.

"Ladies and gentlemen, if all this makes sense to you, then there are several ways to benefit from our compensation package, the best of which is the ability to generate residual income for you and your family."

D. Next Step/ Call to Action:

I like closing out my presentation with a 1-minute story about how the industry has dramatically affected my life. Think about this step before you bring it all on the stage of the presentation. Now that you have done an exceptional job over the last hour, what do you want the audience to do?

What is the next step?

What are the expectations?

Where do we go from here?

Some people are enthusiastic for 30 minutes. Some for 30 days. The people who remain enthusiastic for 30yrs succeed in life.

www.kingpinyin.com

80

2. Enthusiasm

"Enthusiasm is excitement with inspiration, motivation, and a pinch of creativity."

- Bo Bennett

Enthusiasm is defined as a *strong excitement about something: a strong feeling of active interest in something that you like or enjoy.* The word is derived from the Greek word *entheos,* which means to inspire. Effective presenters inspire the audience to want more for themselves in every area of their lives.

Master presenters radiate passion, conviction and enthusiasm. If you don't look or sound passionate about your business opportunity, product portfolio and compensation plan, your audience will definitely not be passionate about it either.

Enthusiastic presenters are more persuasive in their presentation style. Their energy and excitement rubs off on the audience. They are not trying to fake it or exaggerate the feeling. They genuinely enjoy working with their company and believe in the value they will add to the lives of those who make a decision to partner with them.

Passion and enthusiasm is conveyed almost entirely through delivery. Pay attention to your posture. Stand tall with your feet firmly planted and shoulders squared. Your hand gestures and Movement also affect the overall effective of your presentation. Frequent hand gestures are distracting to the audience, but too few hand gestures make you look stiff and boring. Find a balance somewhere in the middle. Your voice is also a huge part of your presentation. Take deep breaths and fill your lungs with oxygen. Eliminate hesitations in your delivery because they make you look unprepared.

3. Engage Your Audience.

To earn the respect of the audience, you must first connect with them!

Great presenters connect with their audience. They build rapport quickly and involve the audience early on in the presentation process. They draw their audiences in and sound as if they are having a lively conversation with friends instead of sounding scripted, intelligent or speechy!

Rules Of Engagement

i.   **Speak to the interest of your audience.** It's really about them, not you or your company!

ii. **Use stories, examples and anecdotes.** Master presenters are storytellers. Share your stories with the audience so that they can connect with you on a deeper level. They have to be able to see that you are human, are vulnerable just like them, and that you have fears and doubts like them.

iii. **Eye contact is an essential engagement tool.** Why bother talking to them if you cannot look them in the eyes? The general assumption is that someone is not being honest with you if they avoid making eye contact with you.

iv. **Talk to the audience!** Don't be shy. Do not hide behind the podium or stand still in one spot. Move around the stage in a calculative manner.

v.   **Smile.** It costs nothing.

vi. **Use names early and often.** Make sure that you provide name badges for everyone. A good way to separate those who are already in the business from the guests is to use different color name badges.

vii. **Be current.** Know about what's going on in your industry and a little bit about what's happening in the country. I sometimes use stories from the news to drive home a point.

viii. **Use Humor.** Do not take yourself too seriously throughout the entire presentation. But do not force it either.

ix. **Read your audience.** Pay attention to their body language. Are they engaged, sitting upright, struggling to hear you or struggling to read the words on your power point presentation slides?

x. **Get your audience involved**. Ask questions. Make them finish off a common phrase like:

"money does not grow on......?"

"if wishes were horses, beggars would....?"

"men are from.....?"

"women are from....?"

4. Be Natural

Great presenters are natural in their delivery. But that comes with a great deal of practice. Their style is conversational and they are completely at ease in front of the audience. Natural does not mean they are born with it. Instead, they achieve that status by working on their presentation Skills continuously.

The worst thing to do during a presentation is to try to be someone else. At best you'll be a fake copy of them. But what I know for sure is that if you try to be the best you possible, you'll make a connection with your audience. BE YOURSELF!

Make a list of presenters you would classify as "natural" and describe what you believe makes them natural?

5. Understand Your Audience

Try to learn more about the people who will be in your audience before the presentation.

- Talk with people within your organization

- Ask lots of questions

- Listen for information you can build into your presentation.

- Do your homework. Research.

6. Practice. Practice. Practice.

"We are what we repeatedly do. Excellence then, is not an act, but a habit."-Aristotle

Practice is a critical component of being successful in any field of endeavor. It exposes areas of weaknesses and strength. The exciting thing about practicing is that you do not need an audience, downlines, or uplines! All you need is the desire to improve upon yourself.

"Every great shot you hit, you've already hit a bunch of times in practice." - Martina Navratilova

Things to work on:

-   Fillers – um, you know, uh, it's like, kinda, ya'll, you know what I'm saying?, etc.

-   Voice – volume, pitch, intonation. Speak from your diaphragm, not your throat.

-   Eye Contact – practice making eye contact when you talk.

-   Gestures – use your hands appropriately.

-   Posture – stand tall, squared shoulders, hands by your side.

The next time you feel the butterflies forming, just remember that you can feed off that energy just like a master presenter and give an exceptional presentation!

"I don't know what your destiny will be, but one thing I know: the ones among you who will be really happy are those who have sought and found how to serve.

– Albert Schweitzer

Chapter 7

Customer Acquisition and Retention

One of the questions that I frequently get asked by guests and many new distributors is whether they should focus more on recruiting new distributors into the business or on acquiring customers. You should do both equally and teach your new partners to do the same.

Unfortunately, many new distributors will focus on the recruiting part of the business with little emphasis on acquiring customers; either because of a lack of understanding of the long term benefits of earning residual income, or simply because no one told them to.

Do not assume that your business partners understand that getting customers is a must. I learned this very early in the business when my organization was small enough for me to know everyone in it. A sharp looking, well-polished gentleman, whom I will call John for purposes of illustration, signed up and was super excited about the possibilities with our company. He obviously had influence because his organization grew to about 38 distributors in less than a month. It was his personality however that caught my attention. So naturally, we had him up front opening up the meeting and getting everyone excited.

Then one day he asked to meet with his direct sponsor who was a leader in our organization, and that conversation forever changed the focus of my presentation. He had not earned any significant amount of money because he did not understand that acquiring customers was such a big part of the compensation plan!

As a matter of fact, our compensation structure, as is the case with all direct sales companies, will not pay you a commission for recruiting people into the business.

Network marketing companies are customer acquisition companies. You get paid for recruiting other distributors only after they sell the products and services in your portfolio.

Every business in the world is after one thing – customers. Your success formula from today should be to acquire customers and to recruit customer getters into your business. If someone wants to join your organization but does not feel comfortable with the idea of acquiring customers, then you should reconsider recruiting them into your business. They have to at least be willing to sell themselves into using the products.

Customers are the backbone of your business. Acquiring and maintaining quality long-term customers will build your residual income. The idea of working hard and smart for a few years to build a massive organization and then retiring with a decent residual income check sounds very appealing to me. How about you?

First things first. Become your own customer before asking others to try your products or services. You cannot effectively market a product that you do not use. Loyalty begins at home. Besides, why should I try your product or service if you are not willing to use it yourself? You'll never see Howard Schultz in a McDonald's drive through line ordering a caramel macchiato! He owns Starbucks! Let the product portfolio be the reason why you sign up with one particular company over the others. Otherwise you will struggle to sell the portfolio and to advance through the compensation structure.

Become knowledgeable about the products and services. Invest the time to read and do your research about them while you are using them. People will make the right choices most of the time if they have the right information. There is nothing more frustrating than a distributor who cannot answer basic questions about what he or she is selling. Your potential customers are looking for a consultant and not a salesperson. A consultant will give you good advice about their products package because he or she consumes the products and has done their homework. A salesperson on the other hand just wants to make a sale by all means necessary. Remember that if you force someone to buy from you, they will never become a repeat buyer and businesses thrive on repeat buyers.

Passion is contagious. Speak with excitement and urgency when asking someone to try one of your products or services. How many times have you bought cookies that you do not need from the Girl Scouts — besides the fact that she may have been your neighbor's daughter? The girls in my neighborhood get me all the time because of the passion and excitement I see in their eyes when I answer the door. How can you resist their charm? 90% of people are emotional buyers. People will buy from you if you make them feel good.

Your list is your working capital. Make a list and always update it with potential customers weekly. This can be the same list as the one you use for prospecting people into the business. Ask them to support your business by becoming a customer, if they do not see an opportunity for themselves in the business.

Types of Customers

There are three types of customers for your products and services. Knowing who they are will help drive your acquisition and retention strategy.

- ⊙ **Potential Customers**: these are the ones on your list who are not yet using your products or services. They could also be strangers who are not on your list. You should always be on the lookout for situations where your products can be the answer to people's problems. Pay attention to what people say and then see if you can add value to them with any product on your portfolio. For instance, if your company offers weight loss products, and while you are at a function with friends, one of their friends starts talking about gaining 15 pounds since the beginning of summer. That would be a great candidate for your product. Do not rush into the sale! Start by asking questions like "Did you change your eating habits?" or "Did you change your exercise habits?" etc. Then ultimately lead her to the point where you are sure that she wants to release the extra pounds — before using your script. Remember, consultants get loyal customers.

One of the products in our company's portfolio is a portable wireless Bluetooth charger. I have sold a few of these while on transit at the airport by simply offering mine to anybody I see wandering around looking for an outlet! If you travel often you know what I mean! There are always people wandering around looking for an outlet to charge their phones! What do you think happens when I offer them a solution to their problem? They end up wanting to know where they can purchase one, and I give them that particular product brochure which has a link to my website! Did I sell them? No! I simply saw a person in need and offered a solution. The easiest way to convert potential customers into existing customers or raving fans is to use your product to add value to them. You do this by genuinely paying attention to their wants.

⊙ **Existing Customers:** They use your products and services. They may even like them, but they will not get on your auto-ship program. There is no product loyalty with these customers because they will buy a similar product from another brand if their supply runs out. They are not interested in becoming distributors. They may occasionally refer their friends to you. It's great that this group of customers is already using your product. However, you want to build brand loyalty with them for your products. They best way to do this is to build a relationship with them beyond the actual sale of the product or service.

Send them holiday and birthday cards. Call them occasionally to thank them for being your customer and to find out if you can be of additional service, like dropping off more products, etc. If they happen to call you with a problem or concern, be prompt with finding a solution.

⊙ **Core Customers:** These are your raving fans! 95% of them will be distributors in your organization. They believe in your product portfolio just as much as you do. They talk about how wonderful your products are everyday on social media. They post pictures about the results they are getting from using the products and services. They will come to your defense if anyone posts a negative comment about your products on social media. These are the customers that you must pay special attention to. They are your business partners. Organize team events and additional product training with them so that you can all continue to grow with your company. In this era of social media, use their stories to create brand awareness for your product portfolio. Respond to their comments on your posts and send them holiday and birthday messages. Take time to organize contests with incentives to get them excited. Share your ideas and business strategies with them because people want to do business with people, not with companies.

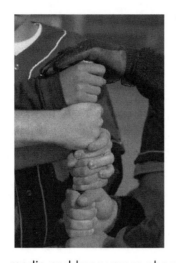 ◉ **Social Media and Customers:** Gone are those days when people used the yellow pages to look for customers. The Internet and social media has dramatically increased our warm market. I have thousands of friends and followers on social media whom I never would have met otherwise. Some of them are as far away as Africa and Australia, but we interact daily on social media and know more about each other than we ever would have if we were living in the same city. If your business is not on social media yet, you need to get onboard ASAP! You are losing out on potential business partners and customers. Social media should be an extension of your brand. You can engage your audience in social media conversation about your products and services. That's why your company, the White House and the pope are on social media. Don't you think you should join the movement and grow your business, too?

Inventory Management: The Internet has drastically changed the way that inventory is managed by network marketing distributors. Gone are the days when you were required to drive for hours between states to pick up your inventory from the home office. Gone are the days when distributors had garages and car trunks full of products. If you are in a company that has been around for more than 30 years, like Amway or Mary Kay Cosmetics, you need to thank your veteran upline leaders for keeping the industry alive! 95% of us would never have lasted a year with our companies 30+ years ago.

Most companies now offer auto ship and direct ship programs whereby products ship from their warehouses and fulfillment centers directly to the customers on a specific date of the month. This takes a huge load off the shoulders of distributors in this era. Try, as much as possible, to get your customers on these types of program so that you do not have to keep a very large inventory stock at home or in the trunk of your car.

"Do what you do so well that they will want to see it again and bring their friends."

- Walt Disney

Chapter 8

Growing Your Business Through Events

Network marketing is not only about selling products and services. It's about people and events! It took me several years in the industry to discover this fact. Right now, there are many people in the industry who have not had any significant amount of financial success, but they stick around for the simple fact that the people in their company have become like family, and the weekly or monthly events have become an outlet from the monotony of their everyday life. Believe it or not, many people do not have enough positive role models in their lives.

Many people are not even aware of the fact that the results they are currently manifesting in their lives are a reflection of what's going on in their immediate world. When you join a direct sales company, you join a group of enthusiastic individuals who will stop at nothing to transform their lives. There is nothing like being in the presence of such individuals because you begin to learn the secrets to their phenomenal accomplishments. I am who I am today because of this industry.

Events are like the heartbeat of your business. They will help you grow your network marketing business to a six-figure income business in a shorter amount of time. Even though you are in business for yourself, you are still a part of a growing organization. Your line of sponsorship and the company schedules events all year round to help you grow your business. This type of support is great because you can ride on the coat tails of those who are already successful in the business until you become one of them.

Types of Network Marketing Events:

Private Business Receptions (PBR)

There is always a grand opening event whenever a new business opens up in your neighborhood. This grand opening event creates the necessary awareness for the business in the community. The same is true for your new business. We commonly refer to this event as a private business reception (PBR), home meeting/parties or grand opening. What's the point investing in the business if you're not going to let your friends and family know about your new venture?

The majority of your friends and family will prefer to come to your home to hear about your new business than to go to a hotel briefing. I first heard about our company at a private business reception. Hosting regular PBRs will grow your business tremendously.

Many distributors will host just one of these events and then give up because the turnout was low. That's why you should host at least three of them in your first month to give your circle a chance to pick a date that works for them.

One of the most successful stories of how you can use PBRs to explode your business happened in the fifth month of our business when we signed up one of our good friends. She had already experienced success in the industry with another company before joining ours, so she insisted on hosting daily PBRs!

We had been doing PBRs every day, but just not for the same distributor! Naturally I thought she was crazy, but an instinct made us commit to what I thought was a ridiculous request. It turned out to be the best decision we ever made because her organization grew exponentially from the first PBR! She reached the highest level in the company in just six months, which was a major deal for our company in those days! If you want to see some momentum in your business, start making sure that you and your new partners are hosting regular PBRs. It might even be a great idea to set a team expectation for PBRs. The real leaders will rise up to the challenge and help themselves to grow in the process.

We had been doing PBRs every day, but just not for the same distributor! Naturally I thought she was crazy, but an instinct made us commit to what I thought was a ridiculous request. It turned out to be the best decision we ever made because her organization grew exponentially from the first PBR! She reached the highest level in the company in just six months, which was a major deal for our company in those days! If you want to see some momentum in your business, start making sure that you and your new partners are hosting regular PBRs. It might even be a great idea to set a team expectation for PBRs. The real leaders will rise up to the challenge and help themselves to grow in the process.

PBR Checklist

It is not enough to schedule a home meeting and leave the rest to chance. The upline leader and the new distributor must stay in constant communication throughout the week for the business launch to be successful.

Every company should have a checklist for new distributors to use in the virtual office. If your company does not have one, get together with your leadership and create one ASAP. Remember that the ultimate goal for your organization should be the uniformity of standard business practices. Every private business reception should at the very minimum have the following:

- Sign-In Sheets
- A TV/DVD player with a Remote Control that works!
- Your company DVD and any other approved video resources.
- Representative agreements for your guests who are ready to enroll into the business with you.
- Your company brochures and any third party documentation tools, like magazines.

- Samples of your company products. There's no need to have a grand opening without the products you intend to offer!
- GUESTS!!!! This is the most important item on this list.

More tips:

- Leave your home setting the same and add more chairs as more guests arrive!

- Offer light refreshments only (snacks, water, soda, chips, and fruit). Now this can be a very tricky item as cultures tend to think differently about food. In some cultures it unacceptable to invite guests to your home without laying out a spread! If that's the case with your new business partner, please let them do what is culturally acceptable.

- Make sure the room is cool. 69° degrees Fahrenheit is a good temperature to keep the guests from falling asleep during the presentation.

Suggested PBR Presentation Format

I like to set the mood by playing light background music as the guests trickle in.

- Serve water or another beverage to your guests and introduce them to each other as they arrive.
- Start playing your company success profile videos as they settle in.
- Make sure that your kids are in a separate room and that they are quiet. You do not want any distractions or running around during the presentation.

- When you are ready to get started, thank your guests for coming to support your new business venture and tell them briefly why you decided to join the company. Keep this under three minutes and let them know that your company opportunity presentation video will do the rest. Remind them to turn off all cell phones and tell them where the restroom is. Then explain how the evening will unfold. I normally say something like... *"In just 17 minutes you will know enough about who we are, what our product portfolio is, how the company compensates distributors and what the initial investment is. Then I'll introduce our guest speaker for tonight who is our expansion leader. He/she will shed more light about our company and answer any questions that you may have at the end of his/her presentation."*

    - Play the business opportunity DVD.

    - Edify and introduce the speaker at the end of the video with a lot of excitement and passion including their pin level in your company, and any other titles or accolades they may have. Always include the fact that they are an expert in your company, love to help people reach their fullest potential in the business, are fun to be around and are making a lot of money with your company already.

- The Presenter then shares the business opportunity followed by a Q&A session.

- Do not under any circumstances interrupt the speaker. Even if you think that they made a minor mistake pronouncing the name of a product or in the price. They are the experts — you do not want your guests to think otherwise.

    - You are now ready to sign up your new partners followed by a getting started training session! This will be a good time to invite those who are not interested in signing up or in being a customer to the room with the food.

- At the end of the evening, the speaker will invite the guests to the next weekly business opportunity briefing in your market.

- Thank everyone for coming and let them know how much you appreciate their time.

Weekly Business Opportunity Presentation

PBRs build into the weekly opportunity briefings, just like three-way calls with your leader to invite your guests out to a PBR does. Weekly meetings are a must for every network marketing company. They offer a more professional environment for your potential business partners to hear about the opportunity. PBRs are usually smaller events and so your guests might judge the opportunity from how many people showed up at your house. Because the weekly business opportunity meeting is a collaborative effort between the leaders of your company, the turnout is usually higher in number since everyone plugs into them. When your guests or new partners go from the comfort of your home to a larger crowd at the weekly opportunity meeting, it stretches their vision causing them to start thinking differently about the business. Many guest who did not sign up on the spot at your PBR, tend to come onboard after they come out to a weekly opportunity briefing.

Weekly meetings also build friendship amongst team members and with other local distributors in your company. A lot of networking happens at the local weekly briefings because everyone in the company attends them. All the top earners and leaders in your local market show up here, so you want to make it a habit to attend your weekly meeting.

Consistency is the name of the game in network marketing. You'll never get to the top accidentally. It will only happen on a planned, consistent action basis. Not having a guest is not an excuse to not showing up either. I've attended several weekly meetings with no guest, but I learned and took away so much from the meeting that not having a guest with me did not matter. If your journey in network marketing is like the typical one, several guests will cancel on you at the last minute with all kinds of excuses from the cat ate their car keys to having a flat tire in the middle of the beltway! Do not let the disappointment be a reason for not showing up. Successful people show up consistently.

When the cancellations and disappointments come, the weekly briefings will help you feed off everybody's energy and excitement about your business and the future. You'll soon come to understand that the top earners heard a 'no' every single day and that they too felt discouraged sometimes, but they used the meetings to bounce back on their way to the top.

I cannot begin to tell you how many 'nos' I heard in the beginning of my journey. No one in my circle had ever succeeded in network marketing on a large scale before. Many thought of network marketing as a pyramid scheme. So I had many rejections in the beginning from within my own family and from my immediate circle of friends who began to avoid my calls! The weekly briefing became my saving grace. I would go there disappointed and come back home fired up! If you are in a bad mood, you need the briefing, but if you are in a good mood the briefing needs you to help lift up someone else's spirit.

Weekly meetings also serve the purpose of enhancing your knowledge of the business. You will learn so much about the company, product portfolio and compensation plan from the weekly briefings because the best leaders in your local market do them. I strongly recommend that you commit to attending the weekly briefing every week for the first 90 days of your business. Just as faith comes by hearing the word, faith in your company will come by hearing the presentation at a weekly briefing on a consistent basis. Distributors who participate in these briefings will grow faster than those who do not.

One the most important skills that you will need to succeed in the industry is team-building skills. The weekly briefing is the best environment to acquire and teach basic team building skills. I'll talk more about team building later on in this book.

Most importantly DO NOT schedule a PBR on your weekly business opportunity briefing night. Many young leaders and new distributors make this mistake. Schedule the private events around the weekly event so that you drive everybody to the formal hotel briefing for a second or third look. Your group enrollment ratio will increase if you follow this simple format.

Checklist for a Successful Business Opportunity Briefing

- ✓ Location! Location! Location! It's all about finding the proper location for your event. First impression matters a lot. People will judge the opportunity differently if it were presented at a Marriott hotel than if the weekly meeting took place at a Motel 6. Remember that you are selling a certain lifestyle through your opportunity, and no one will take you seriously if you are talking about the possibility of financial freedom from a Motel 6 meeting room! Find a decent 3 star or better hotel space for your weekly meetings.

- ✓ Make sure that you have your company banners and signs to point guests to the correct meeting space. This also shows the guests that you are a serious company to do business with. Put these banners both inside and outside of the meeting space.

- ✓ Name Tags should be used. It is a great idea to color separate them so that the guests have a different color from those who are already in the business. The reason behind this is to help the presenters to connect with the guests during the presentation. You can use red nametags for partners & blue for guests or vice-versa.

- ✓ Sign-In Sheets should be created. Just like with the nametags, separate sheets should be kept for guests and business partners.

- ✓ You should also have two registration tables, one for the guests and one for business partners. This will help to speed up the registration process. I also encourage placing the company banners, samples of your company products and brochures, and company magazines around the registration tables.

- ✓ The proper room set-up is theater style if possible; otherwise you can work with the space provided. Make sure that the meeting space has an overhead projector and screen. If there is no overhead projector, then set up a table in the center of the room for your media stuff; laptop with presentation slides and all company slides, the company videos, extension cords, clicker, speakers, etc.

- ✓ If your company offers products, then make sure that you have two display tables up front on each side of the room for the presenters to use during the presentation.

- ✓ Last and most importantly, your representative agreement forms and, of course, lots of GUESTS!

Before the Briefing

- ✓ Dress professionally. Your guests will judge the opportunity from the caliber of people in the room. No tight outfits and super short skirts, ladies! This is a business presentation and not time to fool around. You do not want to distract your guests during the presentation with your outfits. Let's leave sexy in the bedroom and the clubs and bring on classy and professional.

✓ Arrive at least 20 minutes early to meet with your guests. Do not give them a chance to form any opinions about your business ethics by letting them arrive before you, even if they are your family or best friend. This also gives you a chance to complete your registration process before your guest arrives so that you can pay attention to them and make them feel special.

✓ Complete the registration process for your guests when they arrive, collect their name badge and offer them water. Show them where the restroom is so that they use it before the presentation begins. You do not want your guest leaving the room during the presentation.

✓ Introduce your guest to local leaders in the office while you wait to be ushered into the room. That's one of the benefits of local meetings.

✓ Take your guest to the front of the room when the doors open and sit with them in the front row if available. These are the best seats in the house and you want your guests to have the full experience. Do not let them talk you into sitting in the middle rows or in the back of the room.

✓ Talk highly of presenter before the briefing begins. Do not be tempted to talk about the presentation or what they are about to hear and witness. Just talk about the presenters and make your guest know how much you all love and respect that person.

✓ Make sure your guest turns off their cell phone and other devices before the presentation begins so that they are fully present during the meeting.

During the briefing

✓ Be excited, but do not exaggerate any emotions. You can be enthusiastic without being overboard. This will encourage your guest to participate in the briefing as well.

✓ Do not talk to your guests or other business partners while the briefing is going on. Imagine how disrespectful and distracting that can be for the presenter who is trying hard to deliver an effective presentation in order to close your guest.

✓ Do not interrupt the presenter for any reason whatsoever during the briefing. Sit forward in your seat and play team. Participate by responding to the presenter's questions where applicable, but hold all questions till the end of the briefing.

✓ No movements into or out of the briefing room while the meeting is going on.

After the briefing

- Ask your guest if he or she sees an opportunity for himself or herself.

- If your guest does not see an opportunity, thank him or her for coming out and escort him/her out of the meeting room. It's always a great idea to ask them to become your customer and also for referrals.

- If guest sees an opportunity, immediately bring guest to the presenter or other leaders in the room.

- Properly introduce your guest to the presenter or leader and let the leader know that the guest sees an opportunity in the business for himself or herself.

- Never interrupt the presenter when he or she is speaking with your guest. Do not hold up the line when the presenter is done speaking with your guest. Thank him or her and give the next partner a chance to introduce their guest to the leader.

Super Saturday Events

These are training events organized by the local leadership in a market. It is one of the fastest ways to learn a lot about your new company. The PBRs and weekly briefings are short informative events geared toward recruiting new partners into the business. They generally last for about two to three hours. Because there is a necessity to train these new distributors on the system, product portfolio, compensation plan, and on how to grow their business, it is imperative that the leaders organize an all-day detailed training event.

These types of training events are called Super Saturdays. They take the weekly business opportunity meetings to the next level by going deeper with training. That's why you should block off those dates and schedule to attend the Super Saturday events with your guests and new business partners.

I really do believe that these Super Saturday events are the reason why we grew so fast in the industry. We saw the need for training when we joined our company, and as a result we decided to schedule bi-weekly Super Saturday events to accommodate everyone who desired to succeed in the business as much as we did.

If you want to build momentum in your business right now, start with daily PBRs, weekly briefings and then drive your entire team to the Super Saturday training events in your local market. That's where growth starts to happen.

In most cases the local leadership will invite another leader at the top of the compensation plan from out-of-state or they will invite the company founders to build the vision for new distributors. They usually start at 9:00 a.m. or 10:00 a.m. and end at about 3:00 p.m. or 4:00 p.m. Since this is a Saturday morning, these events are always very heavily attended.

The general format for this event is to start with a business opportunity presentation for the invited guests, followed by a break and a series of basic trainings like the getting started process, how to conduct a private business reception and how to acquire customers.

Newly promoted leaders should also be recognized and pinned during the Super Saturday event since it is heavily attended. You should also promote the next big event that is scheduled for your company and encourage new distributors to pre-register for the event.

Regional Events

The company in collaboration with the top-level leadership organizes regional events on a quarterly basis as the company grows larger in size. They follow the same format as super Saturday events but are much larger in attendance size. Most companies will only host three or four of these in select markets per year. They are a must-attend event for all distributors since it is a companywide event and the next big thing to the national or international event.

National and International Events

This is the red carpet event for your company. Every distributor looks forward to attending the national training event because all the company founders and top leadership of the company will be there. The company management goes all out with these events. Many distributors feel like they attending a rock concert! Most companies put together an entire production for the national/international convention. The energy is always indescribable and the training sessions are exceptional.

Many new distributors will put the cost involved in travelling to a national/international convention before the benefits of attending it. I'm here to tell you that you will lose way more money by not attending your national/international training convention as soon as you enroll into the company. We made that horrible mistake when we first joined our company! The international event took place two weeks after we signed up and I counted the cost before the benefit and that set us back six months!

This is where the real networking takes place in your company. All active distributors fly into one city for three to four days to network with and learn from the top earners. The company sometimes brings in industry experts as keynote speakers to inspire the field. I say, if the company is willing to absorb the cost of a high caliber speaker, the least you can do is get yourself there and learn the strategies to grow your business. Let me fill you in on a BIG secret here: your leaders are watching!

We typically focus our attention, time and energy on the distributors who go where we go, because these are the ones who will duplicate us. And while you're there, please make sure that you participate fully! I cannot begin to tell you how disappointing it is to see distributors trying to party and sightsee during the convention week. Plan to go earlier or stay later if your international event is taking place in a destination city and you intend to squeeze in a vacation.

Winners always find a way to win. Loosers always find a way to loose.

Which one are you?

www.kingpinyin.com

"Coming together is a beginning. Keeping together is progress. Working together is success."

--Henry Ford

Chapter 9

Understanding The Team Building Game

If you like to go fast in life, go alone; but if you want to go far, go with a team. Why? Because one is too small a number to achieve success in network marketing. I can tell you without hesitation that this is the reason why so many distributors fail in our industry. Those who succeed beyond everyone's wildest dreams are the leaders who understand how to make this a part of their equation. It is practically impossible to accomplish anything substantial alone. Even Jesus had to enlist the corporation of the twelve disciples to help spread his message across the world. Now, if He saw the necessity for teamwork in order to grow His ministry, do you think that it will be wise for you to do the same? Absolutely! With this knowledge in mind, you must invest time into understanding the dynamics of building a team as you go along your journey to success with your company.

Team Building Strategies:

Recruit Upward. This is a very difficult one for many distributors to get in the beginning. Recruiting upward means to recruit people whom you would consider to be better than you. People whose circle of influence is higher than yours and whom other people tend to follow or listen to. Share the opportunity with these types of people in your life because they have the ability to take the business and run with it to the bank if it makes sense to them! Do not be afraid or intimidated by their success and be tempted to make excuses as to why they will not join your business. These people are successful in other careers because of their work ethics.

Recruit the right people. In the beginning of my network-marketing career, I fell for the idea of trying to recruit everyone into my business. I'm sure that you've been told to do the same too? Save yourself some stress and spend time sorting for the best people. There's a reason why that man working over at McDonald's is still there after 10 years. He has no drive and does not want the finer things in life! He'll even tell you that money is not all that matters after you try inviting him to your weekly opportunity briefing for the fifth time! Leave him alone and start looking for people who are looking for you. Here's what I look for these days as I'm out building my team:

- **People with charisma**. I want to work with people who are fun to be around! Ain't nobody got time for people who whine and complain about everything from the products to the weather!

- **People whose chemistry agrees with mine**. You're not going to agree with everybody on your team as you build your business. Be okay with that fact and look to build long-term with those who want to build with you.

- **People with character**. This is probably the most important thing that you should look for in potential business partners. Some people have no concept of working together as a common unit for the greater good of everyone in the business.

- **Big Picture Thinkers**. I like these people because they can cast a vision and put in the required amount of effort to bring that vision to live regardless. They'll stick with you until you both get the job of making it to the top and empowering lives done. They are creative, and strategic in their execution.

Equip Your Team.

The best thing about direct sales is the fact that you are in business for yourself but you are not by yourself. There are many people who will be willing to help you succeed on this journey. The best team building strategy for leaders is to equip the team for success. Of course, it will be impossible for you as a leader to give what you do not have. Leaders must focus on growing themselves for the greater benefit of the team and that's what you must do. John C. Maxwell talks about the law of the lid in his classic book *The 21 Irrefutable Laws of Leadership*. I strongly recommend that you read this as you develop in this industry. Your team will only grow as fast as you grow. If you commit yourself to excellence, authenticity, servant hood and performing at a very high level, the team will rise up to meet you at the top. Be outstanding by holding yourself to a high standard! Not everyone in your team will agree with you or follow you, but that should not stop you from setting higher standards for yourself and those who are following your lead.

There is no "I" in Team.

That's how championships are won. If you doubt it ask Michael Jordan, Kobe Bryant and LeBron James. You have a major problem if you are the best person in your team. You also have a major problem if you feel that you are the only one who can take your team to the top of your compensation plan.

"Leaders" who are operating in "I" mode will hardly ever grow to their fullest potential because they are coming from a place of lack and scarcity.

The best way to overcome the premature desire to be the "leader" is to know what value or talent you bring to the team, focus on adding that value to the team, and then let the other leaders in the team focus on their strengths.

Resist the temptation to lead from the front if your strengths are more valuable from the middle or behind. This will be a great time for you to pause for a few minutes and define what the word *leader* means to you. A person's understanding of that word usually determines how they run their business or how they lead.

Build For Wealth.

Start off thinking long-term. Do not get carried away by immediate gratification. Most companies offer very attractive upfront bonuses to encourage distributors to grow with the company when they first sign up, but these are usually one-time bonus offers. The real money in network marketing is in the residual income. Take time to study your compensation plan to see how to make it work for you.

I encourage building "Depth vs. Width" if you are looking to leave a legacy for your family. Building depth means that you keep working with your leaders and/or their leaders in each organization until you feel comfortable about the fact that the team is anchored in leadership positions. This is how you play the game at a very high level. You stay in touch until each of your downline organizations has three levels deep of the leadership pin level that you need to stay qualified at your position.

However, all distributors should start off building width before going deep into the different organizations. Building wide will put a lot of money into your pockets in the beginning because you are actively recruiting new distributors into the business. Knowing when to stop and to start solidifying your business structure for long-term growth is the art that successful distributors have mastered. If you stay close to your leaders, they will help you figure out when to start focusing on building depth.

How you structure your business will also determine how successful you become in the industry. Structuring is one of the activities that a vast majority of distributors struggle with. If you are currently one of those who have a decent size group but are not earning a decent income, the reason might be because of how your business is structured. If you take a few days to go through your compensation plan, you will discover what the problem is.

Some distributors do not understand that you need a certain number of frontline recruits and personal customers to grow through the compensation plan. If your compensation plan requires eight direct sponsors, personally recruit sixteen! You'll find out that not everybody that you sponsor into the business will actually do something with the opportunity. More than half of them will not. So building a large team in network marketing becomes more like a game of large numbers.

As your team grows, it will be necessary to have a set of team etiquette guidelines. Otherwise, anything goes. There should be some basic guidelines that everyone should abide by during private business receptions, weekly business opportunity meetings and on conference calls. Teach these to your new business partners so that everyone is aware of how to enforce them. You should have rules about what is acceptable behavior during team and training events. How does your team treat the guests that come out to your meetings? How much should each team member contribute toward your local office space? Who is allowed to present or conduct trainings? It will also be a great idea to enforce a dress code for business briefings. All of this must be addressed so that you all can focus on business building activities and not the politics involved in growing a large organization.

Every time that I talk about team etiquette, I think about **cultural diversity in network marketing**. It will be impossible for you to grow a large team without having distributors from all over the world. How do you handle this diversity in your organization? Diversity comes with its own set of issues like dealing with language barriers and deeply rooted cultural beliefs and ideology. What's acceptable behavior in one culture may be completely unacceptable in another.

Corporations are embracing diversity in the workplace on a larger scale these days. You too will have to open up and embrace the reality of building a large culturally diversified team in network marketing. This will require some effort on your part, but the easiest way to get this going is to start paying close attention to who is in your downline business organization and then making the necessary adjustments to help everyone grow. Ask them questions about what is considered acceptable behavior in their culture and what is not. Ask them to let you know when you cross the line so that you can make adjustments.

Building Beyond Your Backyard. If you stick around long enough, you'll eventually start to build in cities outside of home or internationally. That's when the team building game becomes really interesting and fun if you know what you are doing. There's a lot that goes into long distance building. You have to be ready mentally, emotionally, physically and financially to grow outside of your backyard. The good news for most people is that the Internet has reduced the world into your playground — if you are ready. Your partners in these markets can plug into training online, in their virtual offices, on YouTube, webinars and conference calls. But you will still be required to travel into the market to facilitate live meetings and trainings.

One of the best experiences of my network marketing career was opening up the business in Nigeria after opening up the Maryland market which is one of the largest markets for our company today. You learn a lot about yourself, the people you work with, your company and about the industry.

If you ever get the blessing to open up a country for your company, you'll understand what I mean. But if you've already opened up new markets in your country, then you have an idea about what it takes to get a business off the ground. If you have a business that's already growing in your backyard, I encourage you to make sure that the business is stable before you begin actively building other markets. Otherwise, you run the risk of not having a team when you return.

Team Building Activities:

Running Team Promotions. Your company will run several companywide promotions, but you should run small team promotions to keep your team active and building. You can run a promotion for the top recruiter of the month or for the top customer getter of the month. You can run a promotion for the person with the most guests at your weekly opportunity meeting. Get together with your leaders and decide what kinds of promotions to run and what kinds of bonuses will get your base fired up.

Team Recognition. Babies cry for recognition and grown men die for it! It's unbelievable how much people will do just for a chance to hear their name being called and to be recognized. This is one area where I struggled in the beginning of my career, and if you are a Type-A personality you have a hard time understanding the need for recognition too! Most people have not heard their name being called for accomplishing something positive since their high school graduation! So imagine what happens to them when you give them an award in front of the whole team for achieving a pin level or for acquiring more customers than the whole team! That award evokes the feeling of the pride and joy they felt on their high school graduation day. The result is that you now have a distributor who wants to do more for them and your team grows by default.

Conducting Webinars. This is the information age and the Internet has made almost anything possible when it comes to growing your business. You can conduct several presentations and training events from the luxury of your home using a free service like **anymeeting.com**. Your partners and their guests do not have to leave their homes to participate either. Incorporating regular webinar training sessions is a good way to train your entire organization without anybody leaving home. You can even organize a two or three day training marathon session via the Internet. Webinars are also cost effective for you and the entire team.

Hosting Conference Calls. Just like hosting regular webinars, conference calls are a great way for your organization to hear from you on a weekly basis. We host two conference calls for our group on a weekly basis; one on Mondays to get our mindset right for the week and the other on Friday nights to recap the week and give partners a chance to pick our brains via Q&A. You want to invite other top income earners in your company to train on your team calls so that your team gets to hear from someone other than yourself about how to build the business.

Part III

Personal Growth and Development

If you want success
you must pay
attention to the kind
of soil that you are
sowing into.

www.kingpinyin.com

"Our business in life is not to get ahead of other people, but to get ahead of ourselves."

- Maltbie D. Matlock

Chapter 10
Seven Figure Income Earner Mindset

The difference between a seven-figure income earner and someone who earns $1000 a year in network marketing can be found between the two ears! The quality of your thoughts determines whether you make a million dollars or two thousand dollars in your business this year. It really is that simple. If you do not like the results you are currently manifesting, change the kinds of thoughts you are thinking.

As I network with other top earners in the industry, and other successful people in general, I have found out that they think differently from those who are struggling. I decided to add this section in the book to help you get your mindset right so that you begin to experience growth in your business and beyond. You must be transformed by the renewal of your mind before you can reach the top of your compensation plan and stay there.

If you have ever wondered how some people manage to persist through the obstacles in their businesses to reach the top, then you've picked up the right book. Six and seven figure income earners have mastered the art of overcoming rejection, roadblocks and failures in their businesses by controlling the quality of their thoughts. Anybody who can master these three culprits will ultimately meet with success.

Follow Your Passion

One of the first things you hear from your sponsor and leaders when you first join your company is the question, 'What is your why?' Many distributors do not have a good answer to this question because they have never really given it any serious thoughts. Perhaps you have not either. The easiest way to know why you are in this industry is to answer the following questions honestly. With clarity comes vision and purpose. It will be impossible for you to reach your peak in this industry and in life without clarity, vision and purpose.

◉ **Who are you?**

_____

_____

_____

_____

◉ **What do you want?**

_____

_____

_____

_____

◉ **Why do you want it?**

_____

_____

_____

_____

◉   **What's holding you back?**

_____

_____

_____

_____

◉   **What keeps you up all night?**

_____

_____

_____

_____

◉   **If money was not an issue, what would you rather be doing?**

_____

_____

_____

_____

Keep Your Eyes on the Prize and Focus on Your Strengths

Successful people focus on their strengths and get other people to do the things that they cannot do efficiently. Maybe the reason why you are operating beneath your potential is because you are focusing on trying to make your weaknesses disappear or working really hard to improve upon them.

The fastest way to improve your game is to know what skill set you bring to the table and focus on those things. Then let others in the team focus in the areas where you are weak and they are strong. I know that the tendency is for many 'leaders' in this industry to want to do it all by themselves, but if you look harder, this affects their productivity.

There's a big difference between being busy and being productive. Productive people never try to do it all by themselves. That's not to say that you are going to leave everything unsupervised as a leader. You should always inspect what you expect from your team. In theory, it is easy for me to say this, but in practice you will struggle to get some of the leaders in your organization to understand this, simply because as leaders, the tendency is to want to lead from the front.

Many leaders like to be on stage regardless of if they are effective presenters or not. Our industry is very much like show biz. The celebrities are very visible to the public, but the guys that make all the real money are behind the scenes! So do not fall for the celebrity status until you hit the top level in your company and are making very decent money from your residual income.

◉ **List your Strengths and Weaknesses**

_____

_____

_____

_____

◉ **What do you bring to the table?**

_____

_____

_____

_____

⊙   **How can the team benefit from your strengths?**

_____

_____

_____

_____

Involve Your Inner Circle

When I look back on our journey, one of the main reasons for our success was getting my family involved in the beginning. They did not want to join the business, so we sort their help with my son who was only two years old when we started. Even to this day, my family is still very involved with our business in the sense that they stay at home with our son when we are away building the business. But your family and friends are not going to know how much your business means to you if you do not tell them. So have the talk with them now.

- Who is in your inner circle?

- Have you set the right expectations with them?

- Whose inner circle are you in?

- What do they expect from you?

- Carve out work time vs. family time and let everyone involved know about these set times.

Find Mentors and Coaches

That's how you become a seven-figure income earner! Someone in your company has already achieved all that you are trying to accomplish. The experts will help you figure out what you are doing wrongly and re-direct you towards a path of success in your company. In the beginning years, your mentors and coaches should be in your company and in the network marketing industry.

Eventually, you will need other mentors and coaches for different areas of your life as you begin to develop into a seasoned leader. I've added information about my very exclusive program for entrepreneurs, self-driven individuals, leaders and emerging leaders (*The King Pinyin Diamond Coaching Alliance*) in the additional resources section of this book for those of you who are looking to drastically improve your game to expert levels by tapping into my exclusive network.

◉ Make a list of your top 5 mentors:

_____

_____

_____

_____

_____

◉   What qualities make them your top 5 mentors?

_____

_____

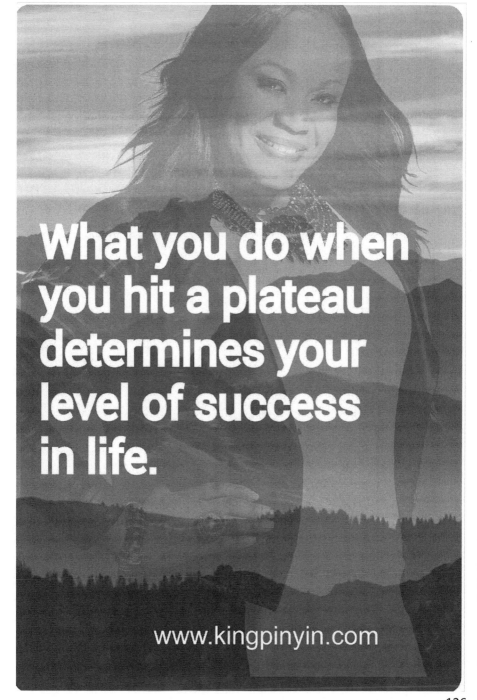

What you do when you hit a plateau determines your level of success in life.

www.kingpinyin.com

Be Persistent!

If you can master the art of persisting against all odds, you'll be a millionaire in due season. Nothing great will come to you easily. You can expect many obstacles and challenges to come your way on this journey. But to those who will overcome the obstacles and challenges, a crown will be given. Talk to your uplines and you'll see that they have had to deal with many roadblocks and were forced to take a detour several times along the way. If you can go from failure to failure without losing enthusiasm and passion, you'll eventually arrive at destination success.

Learn to fail forward. Always ask yourself what you need to learn from the experience and keep it moving. Failure is a great teacher, but few have the guts to let it do its work. I've learned more from my numerous failures than I have from the few success stories I have experienced.

In his March 2014 article, "Greatest Failures of All Time," writer Jeff Stibel wrote about several "failures" that faced rejection numerous times:

In the early 1990s, rapper **Jay-Z** was turned down by every record label in the business, with some stating he was too old, and some concerned that he wasn't "hard" enough, as he didn't rap about drugs or crime. Instead of giving up, he formed his own record label to release his first album. Fast-forward to 2014 and he and his wife, Beyoncé, are worth an estimated $900 million, the majority of it from Jay-Z's empire.

As a young man, **Walt Disney** was fired from his newspaper job for a lack of good ideas. Then he started his first animation company in 1921 but quickly went bankrupt and ate dog food to survive. If you were subsisting on dog food because of the failure of your first animation company, would you start another animation company? Probably not. But that's exactly what Walt Disney did. In fact, he had to restart several more times after that before finally becoming successful. (For the full text of the article, and a more extensive list of failures, go to:

https://www.linkedin.com/today/post/article/20140331213426-461078-the-greatest-failures-of-all-time

Expand Your Mind

◉ **Grow your bank account by expanding your mind**. You'll never drive a Rolls Royce with a Toyota mentality. Once your mind expands, it will never go back to where it was before. Unfortunately, no one is going to grow your mind or bank account for you. You will have to do it by yourself. How to start? Read books.

◉ **Focus is one of the keys to success** in life and in business. The only reason why so many people struggle in life is because of broken focus. Do not try to do too many things at the same time. Remember that you cannot effectively serve two masters at the same time. Stick with one course of action until it becomes successful before you begin to distract yourself with other things.

This business will require all of your time if you want to become a top income earner in your company. We had to put all extracurricular activities on hold a month after we started with our company because we recognized the unlimited potential that existed in the industry.

◉ **Create a list of must-read books**. It's true that we perish for lack of knowledge. Someone has already experienced and written down all that you are dealing with right this moment. But you'll never have the solution to the problem if you do not read that book.

I've found out that you're actually going to read a few books before finding the answers to your problems.

Personal Development Books:

_____

_____

_____

_____

Business and Career Books:

_____

_____

_____

_____

Leadership Books:

_____

_____

_____

_____

Spiritual Growth Books:

_____

_____

_____

_____

- ◉ **Attend conferences & seminars**. Your company will organize many, but you should also attend outside conferences from the personal development experts and success coaches. My #1 recommendation will be **Tony Robbins' Unleash the Power Within (UPW) Conference**.

There are 4 of these per year in the U.S and one in Australia. I attended my first UPW conference in March of 2012 with 8000+ other excited participants from all over the world. I must say that I waited for too long. You should put that on your personal growth and development bucket list for this year.

There are no words to adequately describe what happens at UPW, but let's just say that I walked on fire and it changed my life so much so that I have negotiated a huge discounted rate for anyone reading this book so that you can have the same opportunity and experience that I had. Your life will probably never be the same again after that weekend!

http://www.tonyrobbins.com/special-offer/

IGNITE YOUR LIFE WOMEN'S CONFERENCE: This is an exclusive **MUST ATTEND** conference for every woman who wants to live a purposed-driven life of abundance in every area of life.

I founded Ignite Your Life conference in 2012 to equip, encourage and empower women around the world with the tools, ideas and strategies needed to overcome everyday challenges and obstacles that are the root causes of stress, anxiety, mediocrity and depression.

I bring together a group of dynamic and sort after speakers in the areas of Leadership, Finance, Business, Career Development, Relationship, Health and Spirituality under the same roof for a 3-day TRANSFORMATIONAL event. Go to www.igniteladiesconference.com to find out more and to register for our next conference.

Grow Your Spirit

◉ **We are spiritual beings having a physical experience on earth.** My life changed the day I started seeing myself as a spiritual being instead of a physical being. Whether it is clear to you or not, you are a soul and you have a body. As a soul who lives inside of your physical body, you can be, do and have anything you want in life.

◉ **Your outer world is a reflection of your inner world.** Whatever is going on in your mind will eventually find a way to show up in your physical world. The reason is very simple. The spirit body will always overpower the physical body because it is spirit. So if you spend time thinking about how hard it is to succeed in this industry and how many 'nos' you hear on a daily basis, that's what you'll get more of. But if you spend time thinking about how wonderful the direct sales industry is and how much value you can add to the lives of those whom you come into contact with, your business will begin to grow. Change your thoughts, change your business!

◉ **Create a spiritual routine.** Now that you know that your thoughts dictate the quality and pace of your life don't you think it will be a great idea to schedule time to examine yourself every day? I think it will be a good thing if you can carve out time in the morning, afternoon and evening to check in on what's going on in your thought world so that you can change them if they are not helping you to achieve your goals. My spiritual routine includes prayer, reflection, meditation, and reading spiritual books. Find one that works for you and incorporate it into your day.

You can make excuses about not having the right education, experience, background OR you can choose to TRY. Just try, and if you fail, try again. Trying always beats crying.

~Rich DeVos~

www.kingpinyin.com

"Sometimes you just have to take the leap, and build your wings on the way down."
- Kobi Yamada

Chapter 11

It's All About Taking Ownership
of Your Business

You are in business for yourself, but not by yourself. If you want this industry to work for you, start by taking ownership and control of your business. We often say, "If it's to be it's up to me." Don't just say it; believe it in your heart that you are the deciding factor in your business. Nobody in your line of sponsorship can make this happen for you. You have to get behind the wheels and participate in your own rescue because life is a concrete jungle.

It's easy to think of a jungle as comprised of dirt ground, trees, shrubs, bugs, bushes, and animals only—a place where at the crack of dawn the animals wake up ready to prey upon each other! I have heard it said before that in the jungle, the gazelle wakes up every morning knowing that it must run faster than the fastest lion or it will be killed; and the lion knows that it must outrun the slowest gazelle or starve to death! So it is with the world we live in today.

It does not matter whether you are a lion or a gazelle; when the sun comes up, you'd better be running! Just like in the jungle, life is mostly about survival of the fittest, and network marketing is no different.

Our parents protected and provided for us from the time we are born until a certain age, usually eighteen years old in most countries. We are expected to take care of ourselves from then onward. I like to think of the world as a concrete jungle because concrete is the first thing you step on when you leave the safe confines of your home to take on the whole wide world! And instead of trees, shrubs, bugs, bushes, and animals, our jungle is made up of people, buildings, cars, jobs, obstacles and opportunities, failures and successes, winning and losing, good times and bad times, sickness and health, and so on. In order to survive, you must make up your mind to put your best foot forward once you step unto the concrete daily. It takes the spirit of an achiever to succeed in network marketing!

I learned early in life that to be successful one must think positively about success and successful people. You must consistently hold in your mind the image of what success represents to you. It is very easy to slip into the trap of thinking that hard work alone will make you an achiever. But nothing could be further from the truth.

We started out with nothing but radical faith and a very strong desire to be successful in our business. Then we aligned ourselves with other successful people whom we admired and respected because of what they had accomplished in their areas of expertise. It is indeed true that in "a multitude of counselors, there is safety."

What I have learned and will continue to learn from these coaches and mentors is priceless! No amount of hard work can replace it. Even though I have thrown the word "faith" around casually, it is critical to realize that "faith without works is dead." It is not enough to say you want to achieve success in any endeavor if your actions and daily activities do not reflect a strong desire to succeed. The evidence of a genuine desire to be successful is the ability to exercise self-discipline during the execution phase. For the majority of people, it is easier to start working on their dreams than it is to finish. The tendency to become impatient and distracted is a common cause of failure. The best way to overcome this pattern of quitting before it is payday is to always have a plan and to guard your plan with passion and enthusiasm.

Nothing is as important to achieving success like the ability to chart your own course and to remain true to it. That is why we are advised to "Keep thy heart with all diligence; for out of it are the issues of life", meaning, we must guard our hearts, because the source of life flows from it. If you have failed at any endeavor before, the loss of enthusiasm was at the heart of it, because it is impossible to remain focused on anything that no longer captivates your heart. In order for you to remain true to yourself and to your dreams, you must work with determination and commitment.

I had a major breakthrough moment when I realized that nothing can stop a mind that is made up! This sounds simple, but it was profound. A few years ago, I was at a crossroad between choosing a high-paying job and pursuing entrepreneurship.

I have always wanted to experience life on my own terms financially and otherwise. So I started my journey in network marketing in the fall of 2005. However, as I told you already, we received little or no support from our closest friends and family.

My family, in particular, saw no sense in what I was doing, but most importantly, they did not understand why I was doing it. As far as they were concerned, I had a good job, with good benefits, and a good life! Hence they were very negative toward me and the idea of becoming financially free through direct sales seemed farfetched to them. I naively thought that they would all come around once we started making some decent money through our business. Boy, was I wrong!

When I finally chose entrepreneurship over my "good job," my family was alarmed! They thought that I had lost sight of why I came to America in the first place. But my mind was made up! I knew that failure could not overtake me because my determination to succeed was very strong.

Jokingly, I always say that your determination to succeed should be so strong that the universe is almost scared of what might happen if she refuses to give in to you. "Let us therefore not grow weary of doing good, for in due season we will reap if we faint not."

The top earners in this industry understand that controlling their thoughts and activities today will determine their success tomorrow.

Developing The Spirit of an Achiever

Know who and whose you are. There is potential for greatness in everyone. We are the only creatures on Earth who are created in the image of the Creator. We have been given dominion over the fishes in the sea, the birds of the air, and all of God's creation. We are asked to be co-creators with the God of this universe.

Developing the spirit of an achiever begins with wrapping your mind around this truth. Achieving incredible success will become inevitable once you become aware of the kingdom within you. Just know that there can be no permanent obstacles in your path unless you choose to make them so.

Know what you want. If you want to be successful, developing a definite aim and purpose for your life is a non-negotiable matter. Achieving success of any kind begins with this simple step.

Every achiever starts out knowing who they are and exactly what they want to accomplish in life. Bishop T. D. Jakes had no doubt in his mind that he was a child of the most high God and that he wanted to spread the good news of the Gospel worldwide. Michael Jackson knew that he wanted to be an entertainer.

In an interview with Oprah Winfrey just after winning the 2012 NBA championship, Chris Bosh said that he knew he was going to win the championship from the day he was born! Mother Teresa of Calcutta knew that she wanted to help the poor. Albert Einstein knew that he wanted to be a physicist. Jesus Christ knew that he was the Messiah.

Do you know what your life's purpose is?

If you have not already discovered your definite purpose in life, I want to encourage you to take a few days off and give these questions some serious thought:

- Who are you?
- Why are you here on Earth?
- Where are you going?
- What do you want?
- Why do you want it?

Setting the right goals and expectations is a must for every achiever. Once you discover what your mission in life is, the next logical step is to come up with a game plan. You must have heard it said before that if you fail to plan, then you plan to fail!

Failure comes as a result of the lack of proper planning. Our time on this concrete jungle is very brief. I am yet to meet any human being who has lived for one hundred and fifty years! Yet, this planet has been around for billions of years!

In order for you to make your time spent on this side of eternity count for something, you must take time to plan your life! The plans of the diligent lead surely to abundance, but everyone who is hasty comes only to poverty. "Abundance" is a word that is very familiar to all achievers. They believe in a life of abundance.

As a matter of fact, we have been mandated to not only live life, but to live it more abundantly! Proper planning must precede a life of abundance.

Ironically, many people struggle with setting the right goals and expectations. I struggled immensely with goal setting in my earlier days. The general tendency is to become so overwhelmed with the expected end result that our minds go into panic or anxiety mode. When this happens, we become confused and fail to take action. The best way to eat an elephant is to eat it one bite at a time. The best way to accomplish any big goal is to break it down into smaller goals and then execute the big goal one small goal at a time. "For which of you, desiring to build a tower, does not first sit down and count the cost, whether he has enough to complete it?" In order for you to become an achiever, you must learn how to set the following goals:

Short-term goals: These are your daily, weekly, and monthly goals. What you do daily, you become eventually. The secret of what your future will look like is hidden in what you do daily. Therefore your daily, weekly, and monthly agenda should be based upon what your ultimate big goal or purpose in life is.

Mid-term goals: These are the goals you want to achieve within the next three to five years. They are a build up from your short-term goals. Get into the habit of assigning specific tasks to every day, week, month, and year.

Long-term goals: These are the goals you want to achieve in your lifetime. They are the sum total of your short- and mid-term goals. It takes discipline, persistence, and focus to achieve these goals. It is also very important to constantly review your goals and to take corrective measures as you go along.

If you do a great job of setting and managing your short- and mid-term goals, achieving your lifetime dream will be inevitable.

Guard your passion and dreams. In order for you to develop a winning attitude, you must embrace the fact that you are the master of your fate and the captain of your soul. Permit me to share one of my favorite poems by William Ernest Henley. I believe that his words capture the importance of guarding your dreams and keeping your hope alive.

Invictus

Out of the night that covers me,

Black as the Pit from pole to pole,

I thank whatever gods may be

For my unconquerable soul.

In the fell clutch of circumstance

I have not winced nor cried aloud.

Under the bludgeoning of chance

My head is bloody, but unbowed.

Beyond this place of wrath and tears

Looms but the Horror of the shade,

And yet the menace of the years

Finds, and shall find, me unafraid.

It matters not how strait the gate,

How charged with punishments the scroll.

I am the master of my fate:

I am the captain of my soul.

—William Ernest Henley

Invest in yourself. I can write a whole book about the importance of investing in the temple called *you*. This is one area where the achievers greatly distinguish themselves from the crowd.

If you want to become an achiever, you must sow into, nurture, and develop your mind, body, and soul. Your mind is your most prized possession. That is why your parents and guardians invested so much into you by paying your way through high school in preparation for your adult life.

Unfortunately, not everybody realizes that they must continue investing in themselves past that point. Achievers, however, continue to invest in themselves. Personal development should be a top priority on your to do list. Instead of taking out a loan to buy a car, or using a credit card to go shopping and vacationing, achievers use it to invest in themselves. They invest the money in a good college education, a professional or personal development course, a seminar, and workshop, or conference, books, coaching, and mentoring. "The point is this: whoever sows sparingly will also reap sparingly, and whoever sows bountifully will also reap bountifully".

Surround yourself with other achievers. Iron sharpens iron and success leaves clues. If you want to become a doctor, get into that circle. If you want to become a lawyer, find some lawyers and hang around them. If you want to become a teacher, get with some teachers. If you want to become an entrepreneur, then get into that circle. Your environment and who you are hanging around with most of the time matters! Do not be deceived: "Bad company ruins good morals".

Bounce back from failure or defeat quickly. Get out of the pity party zone and into the no whining zone quickly! Every achiever has failed woefully at something on his or her way to the top. You are not going to be the exception. Make up your mind now to pick up yourself quickly after every misfortune. Most importantly, learn from past failures and never make the same mistake twice.

Trust that God will perfect that which concerns you. He knows what He is doing. He knows why He created you. Be patient and just trust in Him.

Success Profile of Top Income Earners

They think outside the box. The ability to go against the grain in order to get what they want is a trademark of achievers. Conventional thinking is not in their DNA, for the most part. Achievers like Thomas Edison, Orville and Wilbur Wright, Henry Ford, Bill Gates, Steve Jobs, Larry Ellison, Sergey Brin, Larry Page, and Mark Zuckerburg are classic examples of this characteristic.

They trust and rely on their instincts or higher self for direction. I cannot over-emphasize the importance of shutting out all the outside voices in your ears right now! Achievers do not give in to third voices. They are in tune with the only voice that really matters: their voice. However, unlike the vast majority of people, they are wise enough to seek expert or professional advice when the need arises.

They are purpose-driven. Achievers are very aware of the choices they make in life. With purpose comes clarity and clarity makes choices obvious. When you know what you want from life, making the right choices becomes easier.

Go back and review your answers to these questions:

- Who are you?
- Why are you here on Earth?
- Where are you going?
- What do you want?
- Why do you want it?

They focus on their dominant goals and strengths. The biggest misconception among the masses is that we need to spend more time working on our weaknesses as opposed to our strengths. Achievers, however, focus 100 percent of their time and effort toward perfecting their areas of strength. Every human being is naturally gifted from birth. All you need to do is find out what areas you are gifted in and focus on developing those to the highest possible level.

They have a non-negotiable attitude toward achieving their dreams. These individuals refuse to give up on their dreams even when it seems that they have exhausted every possibility. They have no plan B, C, or D like everybody else.

They are persistent. Achievers refuse to give up hope! They are relentless in the pursuit of their dreams. They are always willing to try that one last option to give it one last push before giving up. They know that it's usually that one last desperate push that results in greatness!

They constantly invest in themselves. Achievers spare nothing when it comes to investing in something that will advance their skills. What most people consider as cost, achievers consider as an investment, if it will advance their skills and bring them closer to their lifetime goals. Continuing education and personal development are a must for these individuals. They have learned to grow through life.

They are good at leading and motivating the key people around them. This is a hallmark of achievers. No one can accomplish anything spectacular by themselves. The Achiever's ability to inspire and lead people to buy into his or her vision and remain focused until completion is a characteristic shared by all achievers.

They form strategic alliances with people of a similar mind-set. This could be in the form of partnerships or mastermind study groups. Perhaps you might have heard that many business deals are done on the golf courses around the world. Well, that's because achievers like to hang around other achievers for the purpose of networking and sharing business ideas and strategies. I encourage you to find a few friends with whom you share a similar vision about the future and form a strategic alliance with them. They do not have to be in a similar profession or industry as you are. All that matters is that they want more out of life.

In a nutshell, your success system in network marketing should include books, CDs, DVDs, seminars & networking events. Show up and show out in a positive way.

What keeps you from attracting abundance into your life?
a). Fear
b). Unbelief
c). Feeling Unworthy
d). Negative Thoughts

www.kingpinyin.com

"If your actions inspire others to dream more, learn more, do more and become more, you are a leader."

– John Quincy Adams

Chapter 12

Effective Leadership Strategies

I believe wholeheartedly that effective leadership strategies are the difference maker and the deal breaker in every organization. Using effective leadership strategies is how we grow organizations and impact lives in network marketing. That's why I invested thousands of dollars to become a John C. Maxwell certified leadership coach.

As you begin, continue or advance your leadership growth, the first question to ask yourself is what the term 'leadership' means to you. You may be very surprised to learn that it means different things to different people.

So let's start by clearly defining what effective leadership means to you as an individual.

What does leadership mean to you?

_____

_____

_____

_____

The definitions for leadership are as varied as there are leaders in network marketing and in the world, but it all boils down to the act of leading a group of people or an organization. It will be impossible to build a large organization without developing your leadership skills.

Not every leader that you see in your company today came to the industry with leadership skills and abilities. As a matter of fact, the vast majority of them had to learn and acquire these skills along the way to the top.

List three leaders whom you admire in your company.

_____

_____

_____

_____

What qualities do they possess that are attractive to you?

_____

_____

_____

_____

How can you incorporate those qualities into your leadership?

_____

_____

_____

_____

In network marketing, many people tend to confuse the term leadership with the pin level positions in the company. After all, we refer to these pin levels as leadership positions, so it is not surprising therefore that distributors start thinking of themselves as leaders the minute they reach these positions. The only problem is that leadership is not a positional thing. Consequently, the 'leaders' who rush to attain these positions usually end up having problems 'leading' because their approach is too shortsighted.

You will not become a leader overnight just because you have reached a certain pin level. That will make leadership a one-time process, and we both know that leadership takes time to develop.

If you put yourself in this position where you have to rush to attain a position in order to gain respect from your immediate team and your leaders, you'll be very disappointed and will eventually quit the business altogether out of frustration. I've seen this happen so many times over the course of my career! This does not mean that you should not be competitive to reach the top of the company.

However, the only person that you should really compete with is yourself! I know how hard this can be in an industry like ours, but the beauty of network marketing is that you can choose to do it on your terms. Focus on developing as a leader and not on taking shortcuts to the position. Draw the line when the competition goes from constructive to destructive.

Is the competition in your organization currently constructive or destructive?

_____

_____

_____

_____

What role are you currently playing in the competition game?

_____

_____

_____

_____

What can you do to remove yourself from the equation?

_____

_____

_____

_____

When I first started in the industry, I thought that I could do it all by myself. I soon realized that I had become a slave to my business. If you want to enjoy the time and freedom that network marketing promises those who succeed, you will need to have many leaders in your business.

You can never make someone a leader, but you can certainly inspire people to take ownership of their businesses through your leadership ability. I stumbled upon this fact four years ago when my organization experienced its first leadership crisis.

Up until that point in time, I had mistakenly thought that being there and doing all the work for my team showed that we cared for and loved them. Boy, was I wrong! Human beings are funny creatures.

We are greedy people at our very core and generally think about ourselves before anyone else. But if you take away one lesson from this chapter, let it be this one fact: You must learn how to move people to the next level without touching them. That will require going inside their brains and figuring out what makes them tick!

If you are a leader who is currently having a hard time getting your leaders to move to the next level, chances are that you are using things that move *you* to try to move *them*! But different things move different people. You're going to have to dig deeper until you find out what makes them tick.

To give you an idea, some leaders are moved by knowing that you care about them and will always be there to hear them out, no matter what. While others are moved by not knowing what's going on in the inner circle. They hate the feeling of being left out of the decision-making process. You'll be very surprised to find out that there is also a group that is moved by competition. Whatever it is, it's up to you to discover it and use it to your advantage in growing your network marketing empire.

List your top five leaders.

_____

_____

_____

_____

_____

What do you think drives them?

_____

_____

_____

_____

How can you use it to move your organization forward?

_____

_____

_____

_____

My friend and mentor leadership guru, John C. Maxwell, says that everything rises and falls on leadership. This is so true when you take into consideration how professional sports teams operate. If the team is losing, the coach gets fired! I used to wonder why in the world that happens until I started digging deeper into the true meaning of leadership. If the leader is not effective, they hold the whole organization back. I know that our industry is different because we are working with a volunteer army. But that notwithstanding, effective leadership still plays a very big role in how far the organization will rise.

How To Empower Your Team:

There are five steps that a leader can use to empower the team. I learned these from my mentor, John C. Maxwell. Duplication will not occur in your group unless if you follow these steps.

- ◉ **Developing Competence: I do it for you.**
- ◉ **Modeling the Behavior: I do it and you're with me.**
- ◉ **Coaching the Team: You do it and I'm with you.**
- ◉ **Empowering the Team: You do it by yourself.**
- ◉ **Duplication: You do it and someone else is with you.**

STEPS TO DUPLICATION

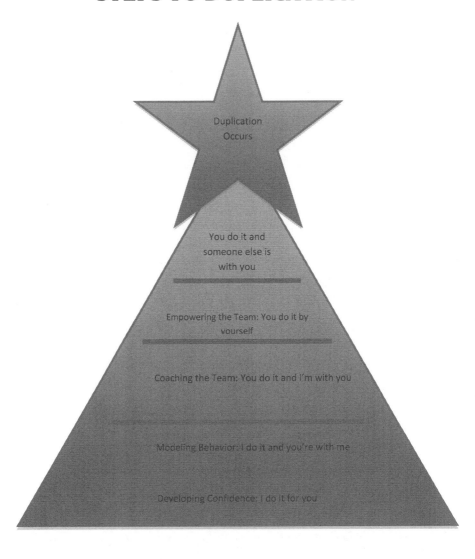

Duplication Occurs

You do it and someone else is with you

Empowering the Team: You do it by yourself

Coaching the Team: You do it and I'm with you

Modeling Behavior: I do it and you're with me

Developing Confidence: I do it for you

You decided who you were a long time ago. You're just living up to that expectation now.

www.kingpinyin.com

Piecing It All Together

I hope that this book has given you the much-needed clarity about the network marketing industry, and about how you fit into the big picture within your company. I would love to conclude by offering you a mini coaching session. I came across a worksheet many years ago by Cliff Walker in *The Ultimate Guide To Network Marketing Business* that I have tweaked to suit my purpose. I have successfully used it in guiding my life and business decisions for many years now. I use it often with my coaching clients to help them gain clarity and to develop a successful strategy in life and business. I also use the results they obtain from going through this exercise to make recommendations about what they need to do next in order to achieve success and balance.

I strongly suggest that you go through each question below with absolute honesty. No one will see or know what your result is. You must answer every question in order to benefit from this exercise. I have italicized the key words in the worksheet for additional reflection on your part.

Instructions: Circle a number according to how much you agree or disagree with the statements below. With 1 = No, 2 = Somewhat, 3 = Undecided, 4 = Maybe, 5 = Totally Agree.

1. I have clearly identified my purpose, vision and goals.

1 2 3 4 5

2. I use these priorities to guide my decision making process all the time.

1 2 3 4 5

3. I have clearly articulated my purpose and that provides focus and direction for my life and/or business.

1 2 3 4 5

4. My *purpose* is in line with my life priorities and is an accurate description of who I am and what I am about.

1 2 3 4 5

5. I have a very clear *vision* of where I will be in three to five years and have put it in writing.

1 2 3 4 5

6. My vision is an energizing force that provides powerful incentives for everybody around me.

1 2 3 4 5

7. I know what my *core values* are and why I have them.

1 2 3 4 5

8. These core values drive the decision making in my life and/or business.

1 2 3 4 5

9. I understand the *core skills* that are required for me to succeed and I am constantly working to develop and improve them.

1 2 3 4 5

10. I know how to leverage core skills into new areas of opportunity in of my life and business.

1 2 3 4 5

11. I am clear about where I wish to build my career/business and I have an effective system in place for generating and attracting new leads in my chosen career path or business.

1 2 3 4 5

12. I have an excellent *knowledge* of my career path/business and I'm constantly on the lookout for opportunities and threats that will affect my career/business so I can evaluate them and take appropriate action.

1 2 3 4 5

13. I have a *system* that allows me to establish significant success in the areas in my life and business where I wish to excel and create effective duplication.

1 2 3 4 5

14. I am able to develop the support systems necessary to service the needs of my life and business.

1 2 3 4 5

15. I am familiar with the groups and individuals who are affected by the way I carry myself and/or run my business and am able to get consistent buy-in to my strategies from all these parties.

1 2 3 4 5

16. I am constantly working to develop true win-win *relationships* with everybody affected by my life and/or business.

1 2 3 4 5

17. I have clearly identified the *resources* required for me to grow in life and/or to run my business to achieve success.

1 2 3 4 5

18. I have ensured that these key resources support the focus of my life and/or business and that I have a regular supply of them.

1 2 3 4 5

Knowing Your Numbers:

- Get your total score by adding up your numbers.
- Divide the total by 90.
- Multiply the answer by 100 to get your overall percentage.

Your total score will give you an idea of the amount of clarity in your life and/or business. The closer your score is to 100 percent, the clearer your life and/or business purpose is and vice versa.

How to interpret your score:

0 to 25 percent = Very Poor. Need a lot of coaching / mentoring /teaching to establish purpose, vision, and direction.

25 percent to 50 percent = Poor. Need constant coaching / mentoring / teaching to clarify purpose, vision, and direction.

50 percent to 75 percent = Average. Need help with coaching / mentoring / teaching to strengthen belief in purpose, vision, and direction.

75 percent to 95 percent = Good. Need coaching / mentoring / teaching to effectively execute purpose, vision, and goals.

95 percent and above = Excellent. These individuals know who they are, what they want, and why they want it.

If you need additional help with coaching and mentoring, please feel free to contact my office at **info@kingpinyin.com** or by submitting a request through my website www.kingpinyin.com.

Don't be embarrassed by your failures. It happens to the best of the best.

www.kingpinyin.com

Acknowledgements

I'm so thankful to the almighty God for the numerous blessings bestowed upon me from birth to this day. Without Him, none of this would be possible. And to Amos, who walks, talks, instruct, guard and guides me daily.

I am so grateful to my calm, collected, incredibly patient and kind husband and friend, Sunny, who is the wind beneath my wings. Words cannot express how grateful I am to him and to my son, Denzel, for allowing me to pursue my dreams without ever complaining.

To my parents, HRH John Sama Njoya & Lucy Njoya, thank you for raising me up to be self-sufficient, and for instilling the right values in me.

To my sisters Jackie, Germaine, Daisy and Claudine, it's hard to imagine life without you brady bunch! It's a blessing to be able to laugh at each other and gossip about the silliest things with you ladies!

To all the mentors and coaches who have helped me along the way, thank you for believing in me. Special thanks to my personal mentors and friends Anthony & Sage Robbins, John C. Maxwell, Paul Martinelli, Craig Jerabeck, Jeb Tyler, Jason Guck, William Faucette, Jr, Felix Fon-Ndikum and Scott Humphrey.

Special thanks to our upline leadership and friends Barry Donalson, C Anthony Harris, Lisa Nicole Cloud and John Jones from whom I have learned a lot about the direct sales industry.

And to Kamilla Collier-Mullin, Jimmy Harding, Luc Tasi, Mary & Tracy Monroe, Achiri Mofor who contributed in one way or the other to the birthing of this book. I love you guys! Looking forward to future collaborations.

To all the many friends and business associates who have come and gone throughout the years; I've been blessed by your presence along my journey in free enterprise. I'm so grateful for the life lessons you've taught me.

And to the most supportive group of family & friends on Facebook, Ignite Your Life Women's Conference, 5LINX and in my downline organization – THANK YOU for your love, and encouragement throughout the years! It's your time to illuminate and shine bright like a diamond in the sky!

About The Author

King Pinyin is the vibrant and dynamic CEO and founder *of **Ignite Your Life LLC Women's Movement**.* She is an author, speaker, success coach, direct sales expert, talk show host and a woman of profound faith. She has mentored and inspired many to reach their peak in life through her seminars, coaching sessions, leadership workshops, *Mastermind Study Groups*, *Ignite Your Life Women's Conference*, Platinum Talk conference calls and speaking engagements.

Her career began in the IT field as a Database Administrator, but her passion for public speaking and a burning desire to help people to be, do and have more in life led her to the direct sales industry where she is currently an elite top leader, mentor, life & business coach to an organization of 55,000+ independent business owners as well as an advisory council board member for the INC500 company. Always the visionary leader, she was instrumental in the company's international expansion efforts into Canada and into Africa as Vice President of Sales.

Believing wholeheartedly that effective leadership strategy is the difference maker and the deal breaker in every organization, King became a founding member of the prestigious **John C. Maxwell Certification Program**. An effective Leadership strategy is how we grow organizations and impact lives. As a John Maxwell Certified Coach, Teacher and Speaker, King offers workshops, seminars, keynote speaking, and coaching, geared toward aiding personal and professional growth through the study and practical application of John's proven leadership methods including *The 21 Irrefutable Laws of Leadership*, *Becoming a Person of Influence*, *Everyone Communicates, Few Connect, Put Your Dreams to the Test* & *Leadership Gold*.

Committed to living her personal, professional and spiritual life at a level few ever attain, King joined the *Anthony Robbins Platinum Partnership* program in 2012. Limited to one hundred and fifty serious players worldwide, the elite members of the Partnership enjoy an unprecedented opportunity to be personally coached by Anthony Robbins, and meet with master teachers from around the world, while traveling to some of the most spectacular destinations on earth. Through this partnership King has access to tools and resources that will help any individual, organization or company to experience massive growth and success.

King is a co-author of *Mastering the Art of Success* with Jack Canfield, Les Brown, Mark Victor Hansen; co-author of *Concrete Jungle* with Bob Proctor, Mark Leader and Steve Rizzo, co-author of *Words of Wisdom* with Brian Tracy and Dr. John D Gray, co-author of *Leadership: Helping Others To Succeed* with Dr. Warren Bennis, Senator George Mitchell and Patricia Schroeder; and co-author of *No Winner Ever Got There Without A Coach* with Dr. Pam Brill and David Rock.

She has been profiled in *Success From Home* magazine (2014) and *Your Business At Home* magazine (2007), (2010), (2011), (2012), (2013) and Women of Wealth Magazine (special edition 2014). King has been a featured guest on *Wisdom Keys* with Dr. Mike Murdock airing on *The Word Network*, Dish Network and DirecTV.

Her mission is to equip, encourage and empower people across the globe to break free from disempowering beliefs and to explore the unlimited potential that lies within the human soul.

As one of the nation's upcoming dynamic conference speaker, King travels 30+ weeks a year, delivering speeches, seminars and workshops to a diversified group of audiences. Passionate, purposeful, motivational, humorous and down-to-earth, King touches the lives of her audiences in a very special way, and inspires them to reach their peak in life.

Her purpose is transparent and her message is inspirational and transforming. We are spiritual beings having a physical experience on earth.

So we can Be, Do and Have anything we want.

It's time to Illuminate and Shine!

Additional Resources

Social Media

www.facebook.com/emeldine

www.twitter.com/kingpinyin

www.linkedIn.com/kingpinyin

www.instagram.com/kingpinyin

Text **king pinyin** to **55469** to be added to my **VIP** Database.

Platinum Talk Conference Call

Monday Nights
Conf #:605-475-3215
Pin #:1032526#
Time: 8:30 p.m. EST

The King Pinyin Diamond Coaching Alliance

Turning Dreams into a Reality by Bringing Clarity and Focus to Your Vision.
-Life & Business Coaching
-Mastermind Group Coaching
-Personal Brand Development
-Strategic Leadership Growth & Development
-Effective Communication Strategies
-Creative Visualization & Dream Realization
-Goal Setting
-Team Building
-Networking

For more information and to apply, visit www.kingpinyin.com/coaching

Recommended Reading:

The Dream Giver by Bruce Wilkinson

Prayer of Jabez by Bruce Wilkinson

The Science of Getting Rich by Wallace D Wattles

Your First Year in Network Marketing by Mark & Rene Yarnell

Think and Grow Rich by Napoleon Hill

The Greatest Salesman in The World by Og Mandino

The Alchemist by Paulo Coelho

Put Your Dream To The Test by John C. Maxwell

Unlimited Power by Anthony Robbins

Walking In Your Success by Rosa Battle

The Power of Positive Thinking by Norman Vincent Peale

As a Man Thinketh by James Allen

What are you willing to give up in order to get what you want?

www.kingpinyin.com

Made in the USA
Middletown, DE
13 March 2015